Delicious Dining Without Fur or Feathers

Meatless need not mean tasteless. And with this indispensable vegetarian chef's aid you'll be feasting on delectably nutritious, flesh-free meals the whole semester, the cheap 'n' easy way, made famous by the original, best-selling *The Starving Students' Cookbook*. Before you know it you'll be making:

- Apple Berry Pancakes • Twice Is Nice Stew • Quick Fix Tomato Soup • Caribbean Red Beans and Rice • Sweet Pepper Fajitas • Mocha Cappuccino Freeze . . . and much more!

With THE STARVING STUDENTS' VEGETARIAN COOKBOOK, you'll never ~

RAVES FOR *THE STARVING STUDENT*

"The instructions are so understandable and easy that any noncook can

—*Forecast*

"One of the most elementary cookbooks ever devised. . . . This time and money saver can help inspire eating habits and nutrition for college students."

—*Changing Times*

"Although geared for the college crowd, this book is useful for anyone who doesn't want to cook and doesn't want to learn to cook, but does want to eat."

—*Blade-Citizen,* San Diego County

Also by Dede Hall

The Starving Students' Cookbook

The Starving Students' Vegetarian Cookbook

Dede Hall

WARNER BOOKS

NEW YORK   BOSTON

Warner Books

Time Warner Book Group
1271 Avenue of the Americas, New York, NY 10020
Visit our Web site at www.twbookmark.com.

Printed in the United States of America

First Printing: July 2001
10 9 8 7 6

Library of Congress Cataloging-in-Publication Data
Hall, Dede.
    The starving students' vegetarian cookbook / Dede Hall.
        p. cm.
    Includes index.
    ISBN 0-446-67675-6
    1. Vegetarian cookery. 2. Low budget cookery. I. Title.

TX837 .H247 2001
641.5'636—dc21

00-068656

Design and page layout by Nancy Singer Olaguera
Illustrations by Mari Estrella

This book is dedicated
to my next generation of
Starving Students' Cookbook users,
Cameron, Madison, Amanda, Emily, and Matthew
with love from Grandee.

Mindi, you'll like this book, it really *is* low fat.
Lynn, thanks for the wonderful tofu lasagne recipe, etc., etc., etc.
Rob, hope there's enough sauces for you.
Thom, try it, you'll like it.
David, sorry, no Cokes.

Contents

At Last! You're a COLLEGE STUDENT, living on your own!

But why didn't anyone warn you about having to cook your own meals, especially if you want a healthy *vegetarian lifestyle*?

After more than 15 years of helping college students get started cooking their own meals, *The Starving Students' Cookbook* now has answered the problems of trying to find recipes that make delicious meals for one, use low-cost ingredients, are quick to cook, and have easy-to-follow directions, all with the vegetarian philosophy in mind. You will see for yourself how easy it is to make the great meals in this STARVING STUDENTS' VEGETARIAN COOKBOOK.

If you think that the secret to cooking is "Let someone else do it!" you are in for a big surprise! Even if you have never boiled an egg, don't know the difference between "fondue" and "Fonda," or can't tell "sauté" from "sauterne," you will love this cookbook. Recipes use terms like "handful," "plop," and "dump" to simplify the directions. Drawings are on every page in case you're not sure which pan or utensil to use. After all, you are in college to learn, but not to spend precious hours in the kitchen trying to make a simple meal just to keep from starving. Money is always a problem, so with that in mind, try a few of these really low-cost meals and impress your friends.

Basic Kitchen Supplies to Get You Cooking

BASIC KITCHEN UTENSILS:

Large Ovenproof Skillet with Lid
(preferably nonstick)
Plastic Mixing Bowl Set with Lids (3 bowls)
Glass 8" x 8" Baking Dish
2 heavy Nonstick Saucepans with Lids
(4-cup and 8-cup)
Pie Plate
Kitchen Scissors
Metal Spatula (coated for nonstick pans)
2 long Wooden Spoons
Wooden Kitchen Mallet (for mashing garlic)
1 set of Measuring Spoons

2 Glass Measuring Cups (1-cup and 4-cup)
2 Sharp Knives (1 Paring and 1 Chef's)
Vegetable Peeler
Can Opener
Glass Pyrex Casserole with Lid (1-quart)
Colander (for draining cooked pasta, etc.)

COOKING APPLIANCES:

Toaster Oven (preferable to basic Toaster)
Blender
Microwave
Oven with Cooking Surface (or Hot Plate if
allowed)

BASIC KITCHEN SUPPLIES:
Paper Towels
3 Kitchen Towels
2 Hot Pads
Aluminum Foil

Plastic Wrap
2 Sponges
SOS Steel Wool Pads (for burned pans)
Dish Detergent

Pots & Pans: Tips & Hints

HOT PANS:
Avoid pouring *cold* water into hot aluminum or stainless steel pans, as they could warp out of shape.

BUY ONE REALLY GOOD NONSTICK FRYING PAN:
You will find it saves you time and money as this is the one pan you'll use more than any other. A better-quality pan will clean up faster and keep foods from burning. Need I say more?

TOASTER VS. TOASTER OVEN?
If at all possible, buy a toaster oven instead of just a plain toaster. You will be amazed at the many meals you can make from oven baked to broiled to grilled to just plain toasting. ALWAYS FOLLOW THE SAFETY RULES on the directions for the oven. Toaster ovens, just like regular toasters, can catch fire if not cleaned regularly.

Shopping List of Basic Cooking Ingredients

And where to find them in the supermarket

BAKING PRODUCTS & SPICES:
Baking Mix ("Bisquick")
Dried Herbs: Basil, Italian Spices, Marjoram,
    Parsley, Thyme, Tarragon
Flour
Garlic Salt
Salt & Pepper
Seasoned Salt ("Lawry's")
Sugar

CONDIMENTS:
Barbecue Sauce
Catsup

Mayonnaise
Mustard
Salad Dressings (your favorite)
Soy Sauce
Taco Seasonings
Vegetable Oil & Olive Oil
Vinegar, Red Wine & Balsamic

CANNED GOODS:
Beans: Kidney, Pinto, Vegetarian Refried
Beets, sliced
Corn Kernels, regular, and Mexi-Corn with Peppers
Tomatoes: Peeled Cut-up

DAIRY PRODUCTS:
Butter or Margarine
Cheddar Cheese or, as needed, Jack or Mozzarella
Cottage Cheese
Eggs
Low-Fat Milk
Orange Juice
Sour Cream
Yogurt (plain or flavored)

FREEZER:
Frozen Fruit: Strawberries, etc.
Garden "Veggie Crumbles" (meat substitutes)
Vegetables: Mixed Vegetables, Petit Peas, etc.

FRESH PRODUCE SECTIONS:

FRUIT:
Your choice of fruit "in season" for best value

VEGETABLES:
Bell Peppers, green (red & yellow peppers only
   when in season)
Broccoli
Carrots
Garlic
Lettuce (various types)
Nuts and Sunflower Seeds
Onions: Red, White, or Yellow
Potatoes, Red, White, or Russet (as needed)
Squash, Zucchini, etc.
Tomatoes

PASTA & RICE:
Dry Instant Mashed Potatoes
Rice: Instant Brown, Long-Grain White
Pasta (your choice, but always keep some handy)

SAUCES & SOUPS:
Creamed Soups: Broccoli, Celery, Mushroom, etc.
Tomato Paste
Tomato Sauce
Vegetable Broth

SNACKS & MISCELLANEOUS:
Coffee, Tea
Cookies (your choice)
Crackers
Chips: Tortilla, etc.
Honey

Jam or Jelly (your choice)
Nuts
Syrup
Peanut Butter
Popcorn
Processed Cheese Spread

Shopping: Tips & Hints

- Check prices against weight.
- Buy small quantities. "Large economy size" is no bargain when you have to throw away spoiled food.
- Buy fruits and vegetables in season.
- Don't buy canned goods that have "puffed out" ends.
- Do your marketing after meals. You'll buy less "junk food" and spend a lot less money if you're not starving.
- When buying citrus, look for smoother skin and heavier weight. Fruit that is drying out will be lighter and starting to shrink, causing a more puckered look.
- When buying fresh strawberries, sniff them. If they are going bad, they will have a spoiled smell to them.
- Check "use by" dates on all packages and follow them.

Kitchen Tips & Hints

HOT OIL:
Don't dump down the sink; pour into an old empty can. When cooled, cover with plastic wrap and discard in appropriate receptacle.

EZ BAKING DISH CLEANUP:
To help make baking dishes easy to wash after oven cooking, rub inside pan lightly with about ¼ teaspoon vegetable oil or nonstick cooking spray and rub off excess oil with paper towels BEFORE using.

HOW TO CLEAN BURNT SAUCEPANS:
Fill pan to cover burnt area with hot water and add squirt of liquid dish soap. Put on stove and set temperature to medium high. When soapy water starts to boil, turn off heat and let pan sit for 1 hour or overnight. It should clean up easily. Really burned areas may take another soaking.

Breads, Breakfast & Brunch

INGREDIENTS:
- ½ cup MILK
- 1 EGG
- 1 cup BUTTERMILK BISCUIT MIX (e.g., "Bisquick")
- handful fresh or frozen BLUEBERRIES
- 1 tablespoon VEGETABLE OIL
- large spoonful chunky-style APPLESAUCE
- sprinkle CINNAMON SUGAR TOPPING (See directions below.)
- plop YOGURT

DIRECTIONS:
1. In mixing bowl, add milk and egg and beat with fork.
2. Stir in biscuit mix. (There will be small lumps in batter.)
3. Very gently sprinkle in blueberries. (Don't mix or you will have blue batter.)
4. In skillet, on medium-high heat, heat oil 1 minute. Pour batter onto skillet in one large pancake. When pancake is covered with air holes and firm on edges, gently lift and flip over.
5. On a plate, lay pancake flat, spread applesauce on one side, and roll up. Sprinkle with cinnamon sugar topping and a plop of yogurt. Serve with homemade syrup (see next page).

Cinnamon Sugar Topping: Using a clean screw-top jar, mix together 1 tablespoon granulated sugar with ¼ teaspoon ground cinnamon.

Apple Berry Pancake with Homemade Pancake Syrup

Serves 1
10 minutes

Breads, Breakfast & Brunch

Skillet
Large Mixing Bowl
Stovetop

Homemade Pancake Syrup

Makes 1 cup
5 minutes

Breads, Breakfast & Brunch

INGREDIENTS:
- 1 cup SUGAR
- ½ cup WATER
- ½ teaspoon MAPLE FLAVORING EXTRACT

DIRECTIONS:
1. In small saucepan, stir together sugar and water.
2. On medium-high heat, bring mixture to boiling.
3. Stir in maple flavoring and serve hot.

Add 1 teaspoon grated orange rind before serving for a wonderful flavor.

Small Saucepan

Stovetop

INGREDIENTS:
- 1 ¼ cups presifted FLOUR
- 1 cup SUGAR
- 1 teaspoon BAKING SODA
- ½ teaspoon SALT
- ½ cup VEGETABLE OIL
- 2 very ripe BANANAS
- 2 whole EGGS

DIRECTIONS:

Preheat oven to 350°.

1. In large mixing bowl, stir all ingredients in order given until well blended.
2. Rub inside of loaf pan lightly with vegetable oil to prevent sticking.
3. Pour batter into loaf pan. Bake in 350° oven for 50–60 minutes, or until toothpick inserted in center comes out clean.

Banana Bread

Makes 1 loaf
60 minutes

Breads, Breakfast & Brunch

Large Mixing Bowl
9" Loaf Pan
350° Oven

Basic Egg and How to Cook It

Serves 1

Breads, Breakfast & Brunch

FRIED:

1. In skillet on medium-high heat, heat butter or margarine until sizzling.
2. Break egg gently into skillet.
3. Reduce heat to medium. Then cook as follows for:
   Sunny Side Up—cook just until white is set.
   Over Easy—when white is set, with spatula gently flip egg over and cook for 1 minute.
   Basted—add 1 small spoonful water to pan. Cover and steam 3 minutes.

SCRAMBLED:

1. Break 1 or 2 eggs into small cup. Beat with fork until pale yellow.
2. In skillet on medium-high heat, melt butter or margarine until sizzling. Pour eggs into pan. Stir with fork and cook until done to your liking.

SOFT- OR HARD-COOKED:

1. Place egg (in shell) in saucepan and cover with water. Set heat at high and bring water to boil. Watch carefully!
2. For *Soft-Cooked*—*start timing egg* at this point and cook 3 minutes (you will probably adjust time to your own liking). Remove to cup and gently crack off top of egg. Dip thin strips of buttered toast into egg.
3. For *Hard-Cooked*—cook 5 minutes. Turn off heat and leave in pan 5 more minutes. Cool and refrigerate until ready to use within a couple of days.

FOR SOFT BREAD CRUMBS:

- Tear slices of fresh bread into quarters. Place them a few at a time in blender jar. Cover and blend until coarsely chopped. You may have to stop blender and adjust bread with a long-handled wooden spoon.

FOR DRY BREAD CRUMBS:

- Lay slices of bread on aluminum foil in 300° oven and toast for 15 minutes, or until dry and crisp. Add bread a few pieces at a time into blender jar. Cover and blend until finely crushed.

FOR CROUTONS:

- Cut fresh bread into ½" cubes. Spread in a foil-lined broiler pan or cookie sheet. Bake in 300° oven for 30 minutes, or until cubes are dry and golden.

FOR GARLIC CROUTONS:

- Make croutons same as above. In small cup, mix 3 tablespoons melted butter or margarine with ¼ teaspoon garlic powder or salt. Drizzle over bread cubes. Toss to coat bread well. Bake in 300° oven for 30 minutes, or until croutons are dry and golden.

Store crumbs and croutons in tightly sealed plastic bags in refrigerator.

Blender Bread Crumbs and Croutons

Breads, Breakfast & Brunch

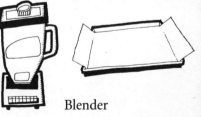

Blender
Broiler Pan or Cookie Sheet
(foil lined)

Bob's English Breakfast (Beans on Toast)

Serves 1
5 minutes

Breads, Breakfast & Brunch

Small Saucepan

Stovetop

Toaster or Toaster Oven

INGREDIENTS:
- 1 15-oz. can VEGETARIAN BEANS
- 2–3 slices WHEAT BREAD, toasted

DIRECTIONS:
1. In small saucepan on medium-high heat, heat beans, stirring constantly, until bubbly and hot.
2. Lay toast slices on a large plate and pour the beans over.

So simple and so good!

Try with English pickled onions *if you want a real taste treat. Wow!*

GARLIC PULL-APARTS:

- ¼ cup BUTTER or MARGARINE
- 1 teaspoon GARLIC POWDER (or 2 fresh GARLIC CLOVES, finely chopped)
- 1 tablespoon DRIED HERBS (e.g., MARJORAM, THYME)
- 1 can REFRIGERATOR BISCUITS*

Preheat oven to 350°.

1. In saucepan, on medium-high heat, melt butter. Stir in garlic and herbs. Remove pan from stove.
2. Cut each biscuit into 4 pieces*. Roll them in the butter mixture.
3. Stack biscuits on top of each other and with sides touching in ovenproof bowl.
4. Bake 40 minutes.

SWEET CINNAMON PULL-APARTS:

Delete the garlic and herbs. Go to Step 2 in directions above.
Roll buttered pieces in ½ cup BROWN SUGAR mixed with 1 teaspoon GROUND CINNAMON. Continue as above.

*Tip: It's easy to cut refrigerator biscuits with kitchen scissors.

Each recipe makes 10 rolls
15 minutes

Breads, Breakfast & Brunch

Small Saucepan
Ovenproof Glass Bowl
Stovetop, 350° Oven

Hot Apple Oatmeal

Serves 1 to 2
10 minutes

Breads, Breakfast & Brunch

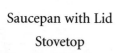

Saucepan with Lid

Stovetop

INGREDIENTS:
- 1 green PIPPIN APPLE, peeled, cored, and cut into small cubes
- handful chopped DRIED MIXED FRUIT
- dash GROUND CINNAMON
- 2 cups APPLE JUICE
- ½ cup OLD-FASHIONED OATMEAL

DIRECTIONS:
1. In medium saucepan, combine apple, dried fruit, and cinnamon with apple juice. Heat on high heat until boiling. Reduce heat to medium and let cook 2 minutes.
2. Add oatmeal. Cook 5 minutes, stirring occasionally.
3. Remove from heat, cover with lid, and let oatmeal sit a couple minutes.

Delicious topped with vanilla yogurt.

INGREDIENTS:

- 2 EGGS
- 1 tablespoon MILK
- 2 tablespoons BUTTER or MARGARINE
- 1 GREEN ONION, thinly sliced
- ½ BELL PEPPER, chopped up
- 4 oz. frozen "BURGER STYLE" GARDEN VEGGIE CRUMBLES
- 1 TOMATO, chopped small
- handful shredded CHEDDAR CHEESE

DIRECTIONS:

1. In a small bowl, beat eggs and milk with a fork until blended and set aside.
2. In skillet, heat butter or margarine on medium-high heat until melted. Add green onion, bell pepper, and veggie crumbles. Stir and cook 4 minutes. Drain off any liquid.
3. Pour egg mixture over veggies. Turn heat to medium and cook for 2 minutes.
4. Sprinkle tomato over eggs and add cheese on top. Cover with lid and cook for 5 minutes. (If eggs are still loose, stir gently with fork and cook until desired consistency.)

Italian "Sausage" Omelet

Serves 1
10 minutes

Breads, Breakfast & Brunch

Small Bowl, Skillet with Lid

Stovetop

"It's So Easy"
Raisin Nut Bread

Makes 1 loaf
60 Minutes

Breads, Breakfast & Brunch

Large Mixing Bowl

9" Loaf Pan (rub inside
pan lightly with butter
or margarine)

375° Oven

INGREDIENTS:
- 3 cups FLOUR*
- 2 tablespoons SUGAR
- ½ cup RAISINS or CHOPPED DATES
- ½ cup chopped WALNUTS
- 1 12-oz. can BEER

DIRECTIONS:
Preheat oven to 375°.
1. In a large bowl, stir together flour, sugar, raisins, and nuts.
2. Gradually stir in the beer and mix ingredients just until moistened. Mix will be lumpy.
3. Spoon into loaf pan.
4. Bake for about 1 hour, or until toothpick inserted into bread comes out clean.

*Tip: Make sure flour is level in measuring cup. Don't overfill.

INGREDIENTS:

- 4 cups regular OATMEAL, uncooked
- ¾ cup BROWN SUGAR (packed firmly when measuring in cup)
- ¾ cup WHEAT GERM
- ¼ cup chopped WALNUTS
- ¼ cup shredded COCONUT
- ¾ cup unprocessed BRAN
- ¼ cup VEGETABLE OIL
- ¼ cup HONEY
- 1 teaspoon VANILLA FLAVORING EXTRACT
- handful RAISINS or cut-up DRIED FRUIT or NUTS

DIRECTIONS:

Preheat oven to 325°.

1. In large mixing bowl, stir together oatmeal, brown sugar, wheat germ, nuts, coconut, and bran.
2. In small saucepan, mix together oil, honey, and vanilla. Stir and heat on medium heat until bubbly.
3. Pour over dry oat mixture and stir until well mixed.
4. Spread onto foil-lined pan. Bake at 325° until lightly browned.
5. Remove from oven. Stir to prevent sticking. Cool completely.
6. Stir in handful chopped fruit or nuts after cooled.

Store in airtight container in refrigerator.

Make Your Own Granola

Makes 6 cups
1 hour

Breads, Breakfast & Brunch

Large Mixing Bowl, Small Saucepan, Oven Broiler Tray (lined with aluminum foil)

325° Oven

Spanish Corn Bread

Serves 2 to 3
35 minutes

Breads, Breakfast
& Brunch

8" x 8" Baking Pan (inside pan
rubbed with vegetable oil)

375° Oven

INGREDIENTS:

- 1 8-oz. box CORN MUFFIN MIX
- couple handfuls shredded CHEDDAR CHEESE
- 1 2-oz. jar CHOPPED PIMENTO, drained
- 1 2-oz. jar CHOPPED "ORTEGA" CHILIES
- 1 8-oz. can WHOLE KERNEL CORN

DIRECTIONS:

Preheat oven to 375°.

1. In mixing bowl, make muffin batter according to directions.
2. Stir in cheese, pimento, chilies, and corn.
3. Pour into baking pan and bake at 375° for 30 minutes.

Delicious with fresh fruit for a tasty brunch.

INGREDIENTS:
- 3 EGGS
- 2 tablespoons GRATED PARMESAN CHEESE
- 2 tablespoons VEGETABLE OIL
- 1 ZUCCHINI, thinly sliced
- ¼ GREEN BELL PEPPER, chopped into ½" pieces
- dash SALT & PEPPER
- handful shredded CHEDDAR CHEESE

DIRECTIONS:
1. In small bowl, lightly beat eggs with fork, add Parmesan cheese, and set aside.
2. In skillet, on medium-high heat, heat oil 1 minute. Add zucchini and bell pepper. Stir and cook 3 minutes.
3. Turn heat to medium and pour egg mixture over vegetables. Season with salt and pepper. Stir gently and cook 2 minutes.
4. Sprinkle cheddar cheese over top. Cover and cook 5 minutes, or until omelet is puffy and not loose.

Zucchini Omelet

Serves 1 to 2
12 minutes

Breads, Breakfast & Brunch

Small Bowl
Skillet with Lid
Stovetop

Salads & Salad Dressings

Salads:

Apricot Carrot Salad with Tarragon-Lemon Salad Dressing	19
Best Ever Bean Salad	20
Coleslaw with Sweet & Creamy Dressing	22
Crisp Fruit Salad with Peanut Butter Dressing	23
Crunchy Red Slaw	24
Egg-Vegetable Salad in a Pita Boat	25
Fall Fruit Salad with Cottage Cheese Dressing	26
Old-Fashioned Potato Salad	27
Orange, Red, and Green Salad	28
Pasta Primavera Salad with Creamy Garlic-Basil Dressing	29
Spaghettini, Tomato, and Mozzarella Cheese Salad	30

Salad Dressings:

Balsamic Vinegar Dressing	28
Blender Dressings:	
Honey Mustard Dressing	21
Oriental Dressing	21
Cottage Cheese Dressing	26
Creamy Garlic-Basil Dressing	29
Peanut Butter Dressing	23
Tarragon-Lemon Salad Dressing	19

SALAD:
- 4 CARROTS, shredded
- handful DRIED APRICOTS
- ¼ RED ONION, thinly sliced
- small handful CHOPPED WALNUTS

In large bowl, mix all salad ingredients together.

TARRAGON-LEMON SALAD DRESSING:
- 2 tablespoons OLIVE OIL
- 1 tablespoon LEMON JUICE
- pinch dried TARRAGON
- ½ teaspoon SPICY MUSTARD
- dash SALT & PEPPER
- ½ teaspoon SUGAR

In small bowl or jar with lid, mix all dressing ingredients together. Pour over salad and toss well.

Tastes best when refrigerated for a couple of hours.

Serves 1 to 2
5 minutes

Salads & Salad Dressings

Small Bowl or Jar with Lid

Large Salad Bowl

Best Ever Bean Salad

Serves 1 to 2
10 minutes

Salads & Salad Dressings

Medium Mixing Bowl or
Salad Bowl

INGREDIENTS:
- 1 8-oz. can GARBANZO BEANS
- 1 8-oz. can KIDNEY BEANS
- 1 8-oz. can BLACK-EYED PEAS
- 3 GREEN ONIONS, cut into ½" slices
- sprig FRESH PARSLEY, cut up (optional)
- ½ cup SWEET PICKLE RELISH
- ½ cup ITALIAN SALAD DRESSING

DIRECTIONS:
1. In bowl, mix together beans, onions, parsley, and pickle relish.
2. Toss with salad dressing.
3. Tastes best if left in refrigerator for at least 1 hour to let flavors blend.

Any combination of canned beans works well in this recipe.

HONEY MUSTARD DRESSING:
- ½ cup VEGETABLE OIL
- 3 tablespoons RED WINE VINEGAR
- 1 ½ tablespoons HONEY
- 1 ½ tablespoons SPICY MUSTARD
- splash WORCESTERSHIRE SAUCE
- dash SALT

In blender container, combine and blend all ingredients on high 10 seconds. Store, covered in refrigerator, up to 2 weeks.

ORIENTAL DRESSING:
- ½ cup VEGETABLE OIL
- ¼ cup WHITE VINEGAR
- 3 tablespoons TOMATO PASTE
- 1 tablespoon SOY SAUCE
- ½ teaspoon each SALT, GROUND GINGER, MINCED ONION
- ½ cup cut-up CELERY

In blender container, combine all ingredients and blend at medium speed until celery is finely grated (about 10 seconds). Store in covered container in refrigerator 1 week.

Makes 1 cup dressing per recipe
5 minutes

Salads & Salad Dressings

Blender

Coleslaw with Sweet & Creamy Dressing

Serves 1 to 2
10 minutes

$\mathcal{S}alads$ & $\mathcal{S}alad$ $\mathcal{D}ressings$

Large Salad Bowl

SWEET & CREAMY DRESSING:
- 2 tablespoons SOUR CREAM
- 2 tablespoons MAYONNAISE or SALAD DRESSING
- 1 teaspoon SUGAR
- juice from ½ LEMON
- ½ teaspoon SPICY MUSTARD
- dash PEPPER

SLAW:
- ¼ head GREEN CABBAGE, finely shredded or chopped
- 1 small CARROT, shredded
- ¼ ONION, chopped into small pieces
- spoonful each RAISINS and SUNFLOWER SEEDS

DIRECTIONS:
1. In large salad bowl, stir together all dressing ingredients until well blended.
2. Add slaw ingredients and toss lightly until evenly coated.
3. Cover and refrigerate at least 1 hour.*

*Tip: Coleslaw tastes best when flavors have had a chance to blend.

SALAD:

- ¼ head ICEBERG LETTUCE, chopped into 1" chunks
- 1 BANANA, sliced
- handful PITTED DATES, cut up
- 1 APPLE, cored and cut up into ½" pieces
- handful RED GRAPES

In large salad bowl, toss all ingredients together.

PEANUT BUTTER DRESSING:

- 2 tablespoons PEANUT BUTTER
- 1 tablespoon HONEY
- ¼ cup MAYONNAISE or "Miracle Whip" SALAD DRESSING
- 1 tablespoon MILK

In small bowl or cup, stir all ingredients together until well blended. Spoon over salad and toss well.

Crisp Fruit Salad with Peanut Butter Dressing

Serves 1
5 minutes

Salads & Salad Dressings

Large Salad Bowl
Small Bowl or Cup

Crunchy Red Slaw

Serves 1 to 2
10 minutes

Large Salad Bowl

INGREDIENTS:
- 2 cups RED CABBAGE, shredded or evenly chopped
- ½ juicy ORANGE
- 1 CARROT, shredded or chopped small
- 1 GREEN ONION, finely sliced (greens included)

DIRECTIONS:
1. In large salad bowl, place cabbage.
2. Squeeze juice from orange over cabbage. Mix well to coat all cabbage.
3. Add carrot and onion, toss well, and serve.

Store, covered in refrigerator, for up to 3 days.

INGREDIENTS:

- ½ cup MAYONNAISE
- 1 teaspoon SPICY MUSTARD
- couple sprinkles "Lawry's" SEASONED SALT
- ½ cup chopped CAULIFLOWER
- 5 MUSHROOMS, thinly sliced
- handful FROZEN PEAS (rinse in cold water to thaw and dry on paper towel)
- 1 stalk CELERY, thinly sliced
- 2 GREEN ONIONS, thinly sliced
- 2 HARD-COOKED EGGS, chopped

DIRECTIONS:

1. In medium mixing bowl, stir together mayonnaise, mustard, and seasoned salt.
2. Add all vegetables and toss to mix well.
3. Add eggs and gently toss to mix.

Serve in buttered Mediterranean pita pocket bread.

Egg-Vegetable Salad in a Pita Boat

Serves 1 to 2
15 minutes

Salads & Salad Dressings

Medium Salad Bowl

Fall Fruit Salad with Cottage Cheese Dressing

Serves 1 to 2
10 minutes

Medium Bowl

Blender

SALAD:
- ¼ head RED CABBAGE, coarsely chopped
- 1 APPLE, chopped
- handful GRAPES
- 1 8-oz. can MANDARIN ORANGES, drained
- handful RAISINS

In medium bowl, toss together cabbage and fruit.

DRESSING:
- ½ cup CREAM-STYLE COTTAGE CHEESE
- 1 tablespoon MILK
- juice from 1 LEMON
- 1 tablespoon VEGETABLE OIL
- 1 tablespoon HONEY

In blender jar, combine cottage cheese, milk, lemon juice, vegetable oil, and honey. Cover and blend until smooth. Pour cottage cheese dressing over salad and toss gently.

If you have the time, chill at least 1 hour before serving.

INGREDIENTS:

- 2 large RED or WHITE POTATOES*, peeled and quartered
- 1 stalk CELERY, chopped
- ¼ ONION, chopped
- 1 CARROT, grated or thinly sliced
- 2 HARD-COOKED EGGS, chopped
- 1 cup MAYONNAISE
- 1 tablespoon SOUR CREAM
- 1 tablespoon MUSTARD
- 1 small PICKLE, chopped (sweet or dill, your choice)
- SALT & PEPPER

DIRECTIONS:

1. In saucepan, cover potatoes with water. Turn heat to high. When water comes to a boil, turn heat to medium and cook 15–20 minutes, or until potatoes are tender. Remove potatoes and cool.
2. In salad bowl, toss together celery, onion, and carrot.
3. Cut the cooled potatoes into bite-size cubes.
4. Add potatoes and chopped eggs to salad. Toss gently.
5. Mix mayonnaise, sour cream, mustard, and pickle together in a small cup. Pour over salad and toss lightly, adding salt and pepper to taste.

*Tip: Smooth-skinned potatoes work best for potato salad.

Old-Fashioned Potato Salad

Serves 2 to 4
30 minutes

Salads & Salad Dressings

Medium Saucepan

Large Salad Bowl

Small Cup

Stovetop

Orange, Red, and Green Salad

Serves 1
10 minutes

Salads & Salad Dressings

Large Salad Bowl
Small Cup or Jar with Lid

SALAD:
- 1 head ROMAINE LETTUCE, washed, patted dry, and torn into bite-size pieces
- 2 GREEN ONIONS, thinly sliced
- 1 ORANGE, peeled and sectioned
- couple FRESH BASIL LEAVES, cut up
- SALT & PEPPER
- ½ 8-oz. can SLICED PICKLED BEETS, drained

Toss all ingredients *except beets* together in large salad bowl.

BALSAMIC VINEGAR DRESSING:
- ¼ cup OLIVE OIL
- ¼ cup BALSAMIC VINEGAR
- ¼ teaspoon SPICY MUSTARD
- couple shakes BLACK PEPPER

Mix all ingredients together in jar or cup. When ready to enjoy salad, add beets and toss gently with dressing.

SALAD:

- 2 cups cold LEFTOVER COOKED PASTA (any kind)
- 1 ZUCCHINI, chopped into ¼" pieces
- handful each FROZEN CORN and FROZEN PETIT PEAS (rinse in cold water to quick thaw and drain on paper towels)
- 3 GREEN ONIONS, thinly sliced
- 1 4-oz. can CHOPPED BLACK OLIVES, drained
- handful CHERRY TOMATOES
- couple handfuls shredded MOZZARELLA CHEESE

Toss all ingredients together in salad bowl.

CREAMY GARLIC-BASIL DRESSING:

- 1 6-oz. container YOGURT
- 2 GARLIC cloves, finely chopped (minced)
- 1 tablespoon MAYONNAISE
- 4 FRESH BASIL LEAVES, cut up (or 1 teaspoon DRIED BASIL)
- pinch DRIED OREGANO

Mix all ingredients together in small jar or cup. When ready to eat, pour dressing over salad and toss to mix well.

Serves 1 to 2
15 minutes

Salads & Salad Dressings

Large Salad Bowl

Small Jar or Cup

Spaghettini, Tomato, and Mozzarella Cheese Salad

Serves 1 to 2
15 minutes

Salads & Salad Dressings

Small Mixing Bowl

Large Salad Bowl

Large Saucepan

Stovetop

INGREDIENTS:
- 8 oz. SPAGHETTINI (thin spaghetti), prepared according to package directions
- ¼ cup OLIVE OIL
- couple FRESH BASIL LEAVES, cut up
- 1 tablespoon GRATED PARMESAN CHEESE
- juice from 1 LEMON
- dash SALT & PEPPER
- 2 ROMA TOMATOES, peeled and chopped into ¼" pieces
- ¼ lb. MOZZARELLA CHEESE, cut into thin strips

DIRECTIONS:
While spaghettini cooks, prepare the following:
1. In small mixing bowl, stir together olive oil, basil, Parmesan cheese, lemon juice, and salt and pepper.
2. Add tomatoes to oil mixture and toss gently.
3. Drain spaghettini well and place in bowl. Let cool.
4. Pour tomato–olive oil mixture over spaghettini and top with mozzarella cheese.

Soups & Sandwiches

INGREDIENTS:
- 1 14-oz. can VEGETABLE BROTH
- 1 small ONION, chopped
- 1 8-oz. can CREAMED CORN
- 1 cup INSTANT MASHED POTATOES (e.g., "Betty Crocker")
- 1 cup shredded CHEDDAR CHEESE
- 1 ½ cups MILK
- dash SALT & PEPPER, to taste

DIRECTIONS:
1. In large saucepan, add vegetable broth, chopped onion, and creamed corn. Cook at medium-high heat just until soup starts to boil.
2. Turn heat to low, cover pan, and cook 5 minutes. Turn heat off.
3. Stir in potatoes until well blended. Then add cheese, milk, and salt and pepper.
4. Cook over lowest heat about 5 minutes, stirring occasionally, until cheese is melted and soup is rich and creamy.

Wonderful on a cold and wintry night!

Cheese and Potato Soup with Corn

Serves 1 to 2
10 minutes

Soups & Sandwiches

Large Saucepan with Lid

Stovetop

Creamy Broccoli Soup

Serves 2 to 3
25 minutes

Soups & Sandwiches

Skillet with Lid

Stovetop

INGREDIENTS:
- 1 tablespoon MARGARINE or BUTTER
- ½ ONION, chopped
- 1 stalk CELERY, chopped into ½" pieces
- 1 10-oz. can CREAM OF MUSHROOM SOUP
- small handful shredded CHEDDAR CHEESE
- 1 cup WATER
- 1 crown fresh BROCCOLI, chopped, or 1 10-oz. package FROZEN CHOPPED BROCCOLI
- ½ cup INSTANT RICE, uncooked
- ½ teaspoon CURRY POWDER (optional)

DIRECTIONS:
1. In skillet, on high heat, melt margarine. Add onion and celery, cooking about 2 minutes, or until onion is limp.
2. Turn heat off. Stir in mushroom soup, cheese, and water. Add broccoli, rice, and curry powder. Mix well.
3. Turn heat to medium high. When mixture begins to bubble, turn heat to low. Cover and cook for 20 minutes.

Makes a really delicious thick soup.

INGREDIENTS:

- 4 cups *total* combination of any FRESH VEGETABLES: e.g., CABBAGE, POTATO, ONION, GREEN BEANS, PEAS, ZUCCHINI, TOMATO, CARROTS, etc.
- 2 15-oz. cans VEGETABLE BROTH
- 1 teaspoon SALT
- ½ teaspoon BLACK PEPPER
- ½ teaspoon *each* VARIOUS DRIED HERBS: e.g., BASIL, OREGANO, ROSEMARY, THYME, MARJORAM, etc.

DIRECTIONS:

1. In large saucepan, stir together all ingredients and bring to a boil on high heat.
2. Stir soup and turn heat to low.
3. Cover and cook 50 minutes, or until all vegetables are tender. If you have time, let soup cook for several hours.

This recipe will make enough soup for a couple of days, if kept refrigerated. Guaranteed to cure homesickness.

Homemade Vegetable Soup

Serves 2 to 3
60 minutes

Soups & Sandwiches

Large Saucepan with Lid
Stovetop

Onion-Potato Soup

Serves 2
30 minutes

Soups & Sandwiches

Saucepan with Lid

Stovetop

INGREDIENTS:

- 1 tablespoon BUTTER or MARGARINE
- 1 small ONION, chopped into ½" pieces
- 1 14-oz. can VEGETABLE BROTH
- 2 cups WATER
- 2 small WHITE POTATOES, chopped into ½" pieces
- 1 stalk CELERY with CELERY LEAVES, cut into ½" pieces
- SALT & PEPPER to taste
- dash WORCESTERSHIRE SAUCE

DIRECTIONS:

1. In saucepan, on high heat, melt butter. Add onion. Stir and cook 2 minutes, or until onion is golden and limp.
2. Add rest of the ingredients to pan. Stir to mix well and heat to boiling.
3. Reduce heat to medium and cook 20 minutes, or until potatoes are tender.
4. Turn heat to lowest setting. Cover pan and warm until ready to eat.

Delicious served with Banana Squash and Carrots (page 114).

INGREDIENTS:
- 1 tablespoon MARGARINE
- ½ ONION, chopped
- ½ GREEN BELL PEPPER, chopped into ½" pieces
- 1 GARLIC clove, chopped small
- 1 14-oz. can peeled cut-up TOMATOES (with liquid)
- 1 14-oz. can VEGETABLE BROTH + 1 can WATER
- couple sprinkles of DRIED RED CHILI PEPPER
- ¼ cup uncooked "Minute" INSTANT BROWN RICE
- ¼ cup SMOOTH PEANUT BUTTER

DIRECTIONS:
1. In large saucepan, on medium-high heat, melt margarine. Add onion, green pepper, and garlic. Stir and cook for 4 minutes.
2. Add tomatoes, vegetable broth, water, and chili pepper. Stir to blend well. When soup starts to boil, turn heat to low and cook uncovered 30 minutes.
3. Add rice. Cover and cook on low 15 minutes.
4. Turn off heat. Stir in peanut butter until dissolved and enjoy!

Has the taste of Thai food with a touch of spice.

Peanut Butter Soup

Serves 2
40 minutes

Soups & Sandwiches

Large Saucepan with Lid
Stovetop

Quick Fix
Tomato Soup

Serves 1
10 minutes

Soups &
Sandwiches

Medium Saucepan

Stovetop

INGREDIENTS:
- 1 tablespoon FLOUR
- 1 teaspoon SUGAR
- 1 cup MILK
- 2 cups TOMATO JUICE
- dash BLACK PEPPER

DIRECTIONS:
1. In saucepan, stir together flour, sugar, and ¼ cup of milk until smooth. Stir in the rest of the milk.
2. Heat on medium high until the mixture starts to boil. Reduce heat to medium low. Stir and cook 8 minutes, or until soup thickens.
3. SLOWLY, while still stirring, add tomato juice. Continue cooking 1 minute, or until soup is hot.
4. Season with black pepper to taste and enjoy!

INGREDIENTS:
- 1 tablespoon MARGARINE
- 1 ONION, sliced
- 1 GREEN BELL PEPPER, chopped into ½" cubes
- 1 10-oz. package FROZEN OKRA or 1 8-oz. can OKRA
- 1 8-oz. can MEXI-CORN (corn kernels with peppers)
- 1 15-oz. can peeled cut-up TOMATOES with juice
- SALT & PEPPER to taste

DIRECTIONS:
1. In saucepan, on medium-high heat, melt margarine and add onion and green pepper. Cook 4 minutes, or until onion and pepper are softened.
2. Add okra, corn, and tomatoes. When tomatoes start to bubble, turn heat to low. Cover saucepan and cook about 20 minutes, stirring occasionally. Add salt and pepper to taste.

Southern Vegetable Gumbo

Serves 1 to 2
25 minutes

*Soups &
Sandwiches*

Saucepan with Lid

Stovetop

Greek Sandwich

Serves 1
5 minutes

Soups &
Sandwiches

Small Bowl

SPREAD:
- ½ CUCUMBER, thinly sliced
- 1 tablespoon finely cut FRESH CILANTRO
- 1 GARLIC CLOVE, cut up (see tip, page 123)
- ½ cup YOGURT
- dash BLACK PEPPER
- 1 PITA POCKET BREAD

In small bowl, mix cucumber, cilantro, garlic, yogurt, and black pepper thoroughly. Spread into pita pocket.

FILLING:
Use any or all of the following:
- 1 TOMATO, thinly sliced
- 1 tablespoon sliced RIPE OLIVES
- handful crumbled FETA CHEESE
- handful shredded LETTUCE

Use your imagination and create your own combinations!

INGREDIENTS:
- 2 tablespoons BUTTER or MARGARINE
- 4 slices WHEAT BREAD
- 2 thin slices each JACK, CHEDDAR, SWISS CHEESE

DIRECTIONS:

Preheat oven or toaster oven to 475°.

1. Butter both sides of bread slices. (Stack bread one piece on top of the other to keep butter from messing up your cooking area.)
2. On aluminum foil–lined pan, place 2 slices of bread side by side. Top each bread slice with one slice of each of three cheeses and top with remaining bread.
3. Bake 5 minutes, or until tops are golden brown. (If you want to brown underside, turn sandwich over and continue to bake a couple more minutes, or until sandwich is browned to your liking.)

Oven-Grilled
3-Cheese Sandwich

Makes 2 sandwiches
10 minutes

*Soups &
Sandwiches*

Broiler Pan or Cookie Sheet
(lined with aluminum foil)
475° Oven or Toaster Oven

Yummy Sandwich Spreads

Serves 1 to 2
5 minutes

BLACK OLIVE & EGG:
- 2 HARD-COOKED EGGS, chopped up
- 1 2-oz. can CHOPPED BLACK OLIVES
- 1 tablespoon MAYONNAISE
- 1 teaspoon SWEET PICKLE RELISH

Mix ingredients together and spread on buttered wheat bread.

CREAM CHEESE, SLICED APPLE & PEANUT BUTTER:
- 2 tablespoons CREAM CHEESE
- 2 tablespoons PEANUT BUTTER
- 1 teaspoon HONEY
- ½ APPLE, cored and thinly sliced

In small bowl, mix together cream cheese, peanut butter, and honey. Spread mixture onto whole-grain or raisin bread and layer with apple.

ONION, TOMATO & SWISS CHEESE:
- splash BALSAMIC VINEGAR
- dash BLACK PEPPER
- 1 large slice each ONION, TOMATO & SWISS CHEESE

Sprinkle vinegar with a dash of black pepper on slices of onion and tomato, and layer with the cheese between two slices of buttered French bread.

EZ Main Meals

INGREDIENTS:

- 1 tablespoon VEGETABLE OIL
- ½ lb. FRESH ASPARAGUS, cut in 2" pieces (discard any tough ends)
- 6 FRESH MUSHROOMS, sliced
- 1 whole GREEN ONION, thinly sliced
- 3 EGGS
- ¼ cup MILK
- pinch SALT
- dash GROUND NUTMEG (optional)
- dash BLACK PEPPER
- ½ cup shredded SWISS CHEESE

DIRECTIONS:

Preheat oven to 375°.

1. In skillet, on high heat, heat oil 1 minute. Add asparagus, mushrooms, and onion. Stir and cook 4 minutes, or until asparagus is tender. Remove from heat.
2. In a large mixing bowl, combine eggs, milk, salt, nutmeg, and pepper. Beat with fork until blended. Stir in Swiss cheese.
3. Pour into skillet with asparagus mixture. Bake uncovered for 20 minutes, or until eggs are set.

Asparagus Pie

Serves 2 to 3
20 minutes

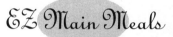

Oven-safe Skillet
375° Oven

Beans and Pups

Serves 1
10 minutes

Medium Saucepan

Stovetop

INGREDIENTS:
- 1 15-oz. can VEGETARIAN BEANS
- couple plops of CATSUP
- small spoonful SPICY MUSTARD
- couple spoonfuls BROWN SUGAR
- 2 TOFU "CORN DOGS," cut in 1-inch pieces[*]

DIRECTIONS:
1. In a saucepan, on medium heat, stir together beans, catsup, mustard, and brown sugar and heat until mixture starts to bubble.
2. Reduce heat to low. Add the corn dogs and heat slowly for 5 minutes.

*Tip: Vegetarian "corn dogs" can be found in freezer section of supermarket along with "Garden Crumbles," a soy-based meat substitute that makes delicious and quick meals in minutes.

EZ Main Meals

INGREDIENTS:
- 4 oz. FIRM TOFU, drained and patted dry with paper towels
- 1 teaspoon SOY SAUCE
- 1 ZUCCHINI, chopped small
- 1 GREEN ONION, thinly sliced (green ends included)
- 2 MUSHROOMS, thinly sliced
- couple handfuls FRESH BEAN SPROUTS, washed and drained well on paper towels
- dash SALT & PEPPER
- 2 tablespoons GRATED PARMESAN CHEESE
- 3 EGGS
- 1 to 2 tablespoons VEGETABLE OIL

DIRECTIONS:
1. Crumble tofu into large bowl and stir in soy sauce. Let stand for 5 minutes while you cut up vegetables.
2. Add vegetables, salt and pepper, and Parmesan cheese to tofu mixture. Mix lightly.
3. In small bowl, beat eggs with a fork until pale yellow in color. Add to vegetable mix and stir.
4. In skillet, on medium-high heat, heat oil 1 minute. Spoon mixture into skillet like pancakes. Cook each side until golden. Add oil to skillet when cooking pancakes as needed to keep from sticking.

Crunchy Egg Pancakes

Serves 1 to 2
10 minutes

EZ Main Meals

Large Skillet

Large Mixing Bowl

Small Bowl

Stovetop

Curried Cutlets

Serves 1
8 minutes

Shallow Dish or Pie Plate

Skillet

Stovetop

INGREDIENTS:
- 1 tablespoon FLOUR
- ½ teaspoon CURRY POWDER
- ¼ teaspoon each dried THYME and SAGE (or POULTRY SEASONING)
- dash SALT & PEPPER
- 4 oz. FIRM TOFU, drained, patted dry, and sliced into 2 patties
- 1 tablespoon OLIVE OIL
- 1 tablespoon MARGARINE or BUTTER
- ½ LEMON

DIRECTIONS:
1. In shallow dish, mix together flour, curry powder, herbs, and salt and pepper.
2. Lay tofu into flour mixture and coat on all sides.
3. In skillet, on medium-high heat, heat oil and butter 1 minute.
4. Lay coated tofu in skillet. Cook until browned on both sides—approximately 2 minutes per side. (Adjust heat to maintain a light browning. Don't burn.)
5. Squeeze lemon juice over cutlets and enjoy.

Tastes great served with Garden Rice Pilaf (page 105) and Fresh Vegetables with Lemon Butter (page 120).

INGREDIENTS:

- 8 oz. WIDE NOODLES, cooked according to package directions
- 1 tablespoon VEGETABLE OIL or MARGARINE
- ¼ medium ONION, cut into thin slices
- handful SLICED MUSHROOMS
- couple shakes GARLIC SALT and BLACK PEPPER
- pinch each dried THYME, MARJORAM, BASIL
- ¼ cup VEGETABLE BROTH
- 6 oz. frozen "BURGER STYLE" VEGGIE CRUMBLES
- 2 tablespoons SOUR CREAM
- couple shakes PAPRIKA

DIRECTIONS:

While noodles boil, prepare the stroganoff as follows:

1. In large skillet, on medium-high heat, heat oil 1 minute. Add onion, mushrooms, spices, and dried herbs. Stir and cook 3 minutes.
2. Stir in vegetable broth and veggie crumbles. Cook for 5 minutes, or until heated through.
3. Turn off heat and gently stir in sour cream.
4. Serve over hot, well-drained noodles. Sprinkle with paprika.

Easy Stroganoff

Serves 1 to 2
20 minutes

EZ Main Meals

Large Skillet
Stovetop

Eggplant Monte Carlo

Serves 1 to 2
30 minutes

8" x 8" Baking Dish
(drizzle bottom of pan with
1 tablespoon vegetable oil)

2 Shallow Bowls or Pie Pans

400° Oven

INGREDIENTS:

- 1 EGGPLANT, cut into about 10 half-inch slices
- 5 tablespoons PIZZA SAUCE
- 5 slices MOZZARELLA CHEESE, cut to fit eggplant slices
- 1 EGG
- 1 tablespoon MILK
- 12 SALTINE CRACKERS, crushed into crumbs
- pinch each dried BASIL, TARRAGON, and PARSLEY
- BLACK PEPPER to taste
- 1 ½ tablespoons VEGETABLE OIL

DIRECTIONS:

Preheat oven to 400°.

1. On each of 5 slices of eggplant, spread 1 tablespoon pizza sauce and top with 1 slice cheese. Cover each with remaining eggplant.
2. In a shallow bowl, beat egg and milk with fork.
3. In second shallow bowl, stir together cracker crumbs with herbs and spice.
4. Dip each eggplant "sandwich" into egg mixture, then into crumb mixture, turning to coat both sides. (Press crumb mixture into and around edges to coat entire sandwich.)
5. In baking dish, lay eggplant and drizzle with vegetable oil.
6. Cover pan with aluminum foil. Bake 20 minutes. Remove foil and turn eggplant over. Bake until eggplant is tender, about 10 minutes.

INGREDIENTS:
- 1 tablespoon VEGETABLE or OLIVE OIL
- ½ ONION, chopped
- 2 GARLIC cloves, finely chopped (see tip, page 123)
- small JALAPEÑO CHILI, cut up small
- 1 14-oz. can VEGETABLE BROTH
- 1 ZUCCHINI, thinly sliced
- 1 YELLOW CROOKNECK SQUASH, thinly sliced
- 1 8-oz. can MEXI-CORN (corn kernels with peppers)
- 1 8-oz. can RED KIDNEY BEANS
- 1 8-oz. can GREEN BEANS

DIRECTIONS:
1. In large saucepan, heat oil on high heat 1 minute. Add onion, garlic, and chili. Stir and cook 2 minutes, or until onion is limp.
2. Add vegetable broth and squash. Reduce heat to medium high, cover, and cook 10 minutes.
3. Stir in corn and beans. Reduce heat to medium low, cover, and cook slowly 10 minutes, or until heated throughout.

Serve in a large French roll, scooped out like a canoe, creating a delicious edible bowl.

Just Right Bean Stew

Serves 2 to 3
30 minutes

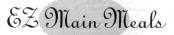

Large Saucepan with Lid
Stovetop

Mashed Potato Casserole

Serves 1 to 2
45 minutes

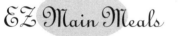

Medium Saucepan

8" x 8" Baking Pan (rubbed lightly with cooking oil or nonstick cooking spray)

350° Oven

INGREDIENTS:
- 1 cup WATER
- ⅓ cup MILK
- 2 tablespoons BUTTER or MARGARINE
- ½ teaspoon SALT
- 1 ⅓ cups INSTANT MASHED POTATOES
- ½ cup SOUR CREAM
- ½ cup shredded CHEDDAR CHEESE
- 8 oz. frozen "BURGER STYLE" VEGGIE CRUMBLES
- ½ cup shredded MOZZARELLA CHEESE
- 1 tablespoon GRATED PARMESAN CHEESE

DIRECTIONS:

Preheat oven to 350°.

1. In 2-quart saucepan, on medium-high heat, add water, milk, margarine, and salt. Stir and heat just until beginning to boil.
2. Remove pan from heat and stir in potatoes just until moistened. Let stand about 30 seconds, or until liquid is absorbed. Whip with fork until fluffy. Stir in sour cream and Cheddar cheese.
3. In baking pan, spread layers of half of potato mixture, veggie crumbles, mozzarella cheese, and rest of potato mixture. Top with Parmesan cheese.
4. Bake uncovered for 25 minutes, or until light brown.

INGREDIENTS:
- 1 8-oz. can CREAMED CORN
- 1 8-oz. can WHOLE KERNEL CORN
- 4 oz. SOUR CREAM
- 1 small box CORN MUFFIN MIX (e.g., "Jiffy")
- 2 EGGS
- 1 cup shredded CHEDDAR CHEESE

DIRECTIONS:

Preheat oven to 350°.

1. In baking dish, dump all ingredients together except cheese.
2. Stir to mix well.
3. Top with cheese.
4. Bake for 1 hour.

Fresh fruit salad goes well with this meal.

Mindi's Iowa Corn Bake

Serves 2 to 3
70 minutes

EZ Main Meals

Medium Bowl
8" x 8" Baking Dish
350° Oven

Peppers, Peanuts & Spinach

Serves 1
10 minutes

EZ Main Meals

Skillet with Lid

Stovetop

INGREDIENTS:
- 1 tablespoon OLIVE or VEGETABLE OIL
- ¼ ONION, cut into thin slices
- ½ GREEN BELL PEPPER, cored and cut lengthwise into strips
- 1 TOMATO, cut up
- ½ lb. FRESH SPINACH, washed well*
- ¼ teaspoon GARLIC SALT
- dash BLACK PEPPER
- 2 tablespoons PEANUT BUTTER

DIRECTIONS:
1. In skillet, on high heat, heat oil 1 minute. Add onion and green pepper. Cook and stir 2 minutes, or until onion is limp.
2. Stir in tomato, spinach, garlic salt, and pepper. Turn heat to medium, cover, and cook 5 minutes.
3. Stir in peanut butter.

Delicious dish served with steamed rice and fresh fruit.

*Tip: To wash spinach, soak in sink filled with cold water for a few minutes, allowing dirt to fall to bottom. Gently remove and lay on a couple of paper towels. Roll up tightly and squeeze excess water out.

INGREDIENTS:
- 1 tablespoon OLIVE OIL
- 1 large PORTOBELLO MUSHROOM, stem removed
- sprinkle GARLIC SALT
- couple splashes WORCESTERSHIRE SAUCE
- sprig PARSLEY, cut up
- 1 slice SWISS CHEESE
- 1 HAMBURGER BUN

DIRECTIONS:
1. In skillet, on medium-high heat, heat oil 1 minute.
2. Lay mushroom in pan and sprinkle with garlic salt, Worcestershire sauce, and parsley.
3. Cook 2 minutes on each side, or until lightly browned.
4. Cover pan, lower heat to medium, and cook 5 minutes.
5. Place cheese over mushroom. Cover and cook for 1 minute, or until cheese melts.

Serve on a buttered hamburger bun, adding your choice of condiments.

Portobello Mushroom
Gourmet Burger

Serves 1
10 minutes

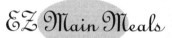

Skillet with Lid

Stovetop

Quick & Easy
Vegetable Pie

Serves 1 to 2
25 minutes

EZ Main Meals

8" x 8" Baking Pan (lightly
rubbed with vegetable oil or
nonstick cooking spray)

Small Bowl

375° Oven

INGREDIENTS:
- 1 10-oz. package FROZEN MIXED VEGETABLES
- 4 MUSHROOMS, sliced
- 1 GARLIC CLOVE, cut into small pieces
- couple pinches each DRIED BASIL and DRIED OREGANO
- dash SALT & PEPPER
- 1 10-oz. can CREAM OF CELERY SOUP
- 2 tablespoons MILK
- ½ cup shredded CHEDDAR CHEESE
- ½ 8-oz. bag FROZEN "TATER TOTS"

DIRECTIONS:
Preheat oven to 375°.
1. In baking dish, mix together the vegetables, mushrooms, garlic, and herbs and salt and pepper.
2. In small bowl, stir soup with milk until smooth. Pour over vegetable mixture. Sprinkle cheese over vegetables.
3. Place "Tater Tots" on top of the cheese with sides touching.
4. Bake for 25 minutes, or until "Tater Tots" are crisp and brown on top.

INGREDIENTS:

- 2 GREEN BELL PEPPERS, tops cut off and seeds removed[*]
- 1 cup INSTANT BROWN RICE, cooked according to package directions
- 2 GREEN ONIONS, thinly sliced (greens included)
- handful FROZEN GREEN PEAS
- 1 15-oz. can cut-up stewed TOMATOES, drained
- couple shakes GRATED PARMESAN CHEESE

DIRECTIONS:

Preheat oven to 350°.

1. In baking dish, add water to about ½" depth. Stand peppers in water and place pan in center of oven. Let peppers precook for 15 minutes while you cook the rice.
2. When rice is cooked, stir in green onions, frozen peas, and drained tomatoes. Stir to mix well.
3. Remove peppers from oven and fill cavities with rice mixture.
4. Set filled peppers back in hot water and return pan to oven. Cook, uncovered, 15 minutes.
5. Sprinkle with Parmesan cheese and enjoy.

[*]*To Prepare Bell Peppers:* Cut tops off, leaving large hole in top only. Remove all seeds and membrane. Peppers should stand by themselves; don't cut off bottoms.

Stuffed Green Peppers

Serves 1
40 minutes

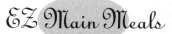

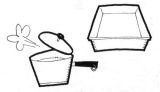

8" x 8" Baking Dish
Saucepan with Lid
350° Oven

Thom's Marinated Peppers and Pineapple

Serves 1 to 2
30 minutes

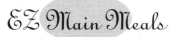

Skillet
Stovetop

MARINADE:
- 1 6-oz. can PINEAPPLE JUICE (If using pineapple chunks in a 15-oz. can, drain off pineapple juice and use in marinade.)
- 3 teaspoons SOY SAUCE
- 2 teaspoons GARLIC POWDER or 1 large GARLIC CLOVE, cut into tiny pieces
- ½ teaspoon POWDERED GINGER or grated FRESH GINGER

Combine all ingredients in a sealproof plastic bag. Squish to blend flavors and refrigerate until ready to use. (Keeps for 1 week.)

HAWAIIAN PEPPERS AND PINEAPPLE:
- 1 GREEN BELL PEPPER, thinly sliced
- ½ ONION, thinly sliced
- 10 small WHOLE MUSHROOMS, washed well
- 1 15-oz. can PINEAPPLE CHUNKS, well drained, or FRESH PINEAPPLE, cut up

DIRECTIONS:
1. Dump all ingredients into bag of marinade. Let sit for 1 hour.
2. In skillet, on high heat, add vegetables and marinade sauce. Cook and stir 4 minutes, or until vegetables are tender but still crisp.

Delicious over hot rice and sprinkled with shredded coconut!

INGREDIENTS:

- 1 tablespoon VEGETABLE OIL
- ½ ONION, chopped
- 2 GARLIC CLOVES, cut into tiny pieces
- couple pinches any or all of following HERBS: PARSLEY, BASIL, MARJO-RAM, THYME, ROSEMARY, TARRAGON
- 2 POTATOES, cut crosswise in ¼" slices
- 2 cups any *leftover* COOKED VEGETABLES
- 1 10-oz. can CREAM MUSHROOM SOUP
- 2 cups WATER
- splash RED WINE

DIRECTIONS:

1. In skillet, on high heat, heat oil for 1 minute. Add onion, garlic, and herbs. Stir and cook for 2 minutes. Add potatoes and cook 5 minutes.
2. Dump in rest of vegetables. Add soup, water, and wine. Stir to blend liquids.
3. Turn heat to medium low and cover pan with lid. Cook 15 minutes, or until heated through and potatoes are tender.

Fabulous with warm French bread.

Twice Is Nice Stew

Serves 1 to 2
25 minutes

EZ Main Meals (with Leftovers)

Large Skillet with Lid
Stovetop

Main Meals Mexican Style

INGREDIENTS:

- ½ cup uncooked FROZEN CORN KERNELS
- ½ 4-oz. can CUT-UP GREEN "ORTEGA" CHILIES
- ½ cup GREEN SALSA
- 1 15-oz. can BLACK BEANS, drained
- 4 oz. FIRM TOFU, drained and patted dry with paper towels
- couple handfuls TORTILLA CHIPS
- desired condiments: SHREDDED CHEESE, SOUR CREAM, GUA-CAMOLE, etc.

DIRECTIONS:

1. In medium saucepan, on medium-high heat, stir in corn, chilies, salsa, and drained black beans. Cook about 8 minutes, or until corn is cooked.
2. With fork, mash tofu to a soft and smooth paste. Add to vegetables and continue to cook 10 minutes until all is hot.
3. Serve over tortilla chips and top with your choice of condiments.

Black Bean and Tofu Tostada

Serves 2 to 3
20 minutes

*Main Meals
Mexican Style*

Medium Saucepan
Stovetop

Cheap Chili & Chips

Serves 1 to 2
15 minutes

Main Meals
Mexican Style

Saucepan with Lid

Stovetop

INGREDIENTS:

- 1 8-oz. can RED KIDNEY BEANS with liquid
- ¼ cup BARBECUE SAUCE
- ½ package dry CHILI SEASONING MIX
- couple handfuls CORN CHIPS, crushed
- couple handfuls shredded CHEDDAR CHEESE
- plop SOUR CREAM
- couple spoonfuls SALSA

DIRECTIONS:

1. In saucepan, on medium heat, stir together beans, barbecue sauce, and chili seasoning. Cover and heat 15 minutes, stirring occasionally.
2. Spread crushed corn chips on dinner plate.
3. Pour bean mixture over top and sprinkle with cheese.
4. Top with sour cream and salsa.

If fresh avocado is available and inexpensive, cut up one half avocado and heap it on top.

INGREDIENTS:
- 1 tablespoon VEGETABLE OIL
- 4 oz. frozen "BURGER STYLE" VEGGIE CRUMBLES
- ¼ GREEN BELL PEPPER, chopped small
- ¼ ONION, chopped
- 3–4 READY-MADE TACO SHELLS
- handful shredded CHEDDAR CHEESE
- ¼ head LETTUCE, shredded
- 1 large TOMATO, chopped
- splash SALSA or "Tabasco" HOT SAUCE

DIRECTIONS:
1. In skillet, on medium-high heat, heat oil 1 minute. Stir in veggie crumbles, bell pepper, and onion. Cook 5 minutes.
2. Lightly warm "ready-made" taco shells in 350° oven or toaster oven for a few minutes until warm.
3. Place veggie crumbles, cheese, shredded lettuce, and tomato in warm taco shells and add salsa or hot sauce.

Cheater's Tacos

Serves 1
8 minutes

*Main Meals
Mexican Style*

Skillet
Stovetop,
350° Oven, or
Toaster Oven

Chilis Rellenos

Serves 1
20 minutes

Main Meals
Mexican Style

Medium Mixing Bowl

8" x 8" Baking Pan (rubbed lightly with cooking oil to prevent sticking)

400° Oven

INGREDIENTS:
- 1 4-oz. can whole GREEN CHILIES
- 2 cups shredded CHEDDAR CHEESE
- 1 EGG
- ½ cup MILK
- ¼ cup BAKING MIX (e.g., "Bisquick")

DIRECTIONS:

Preheat oven to 400°.

1. Open chili peppers lengthwise and remove seeds.
2. In baking dish, lay chili peppers flat and sprinkle with shredded cheese.
3. In mixing bowl, lightly beat egg with fork. Add milk and baking mix and stir. (Batter will be slightly lumpy, but no big globs, please.)
4. Pour over peppers and cheese.
5. Bake for 30 minutes, or until puffy and golden.

Great with Orange, Red, and Green Salad (page 28).

INGREDIENTS:
- 2 large FLOUR TORTILLAS
- 1 tablespoon VEGETABLE OIL
- ¼ ONION, chopped
- 4 MUSHROOMS, sliced
- ¼ GREEN BELL PEPPER, sliced into very thin strips
- 1 small ZUCCHINI, thinly sliced
- 1 CARROT, cut crosswise in thin slices
- fresh CILANTRO, finely chopped
- dash SALT & PEPPER
- couple handfuls shredded JACK CHEESE

DIRECTIONS:

Preheat oven to 450°.

1. On broiler pan, lay tortillas flat and bake in hot oven for 2 minutes. Remove pan from the oven and set aside to be used later.
2. In large skillet, heat the oil on medium-high heat 1 minute. Add onion, mushrooms, bell pepper, zucchini, carrot, and cilantro. Stir and cook for about 10 minutes, or until vegetables are brown and moisture is gone from pan. (Drain off any excess liquid.)
3. Spoon vegetables over tortillas on broiler pan, season with salt and pepper, and sprinkle with cheese. (Don't roll up.)
4. Return to hot oven and bake for 1–2 minutes, or just until cheese is melted.

Mushroom Tostadas

Serves 1
20 minutes

Main Meals
Mexican Style

Oven Broiler Pan (lined with aluminum foil)

Large Skillet

450° Oven

Sweet Pepper Fajitas

Serves 1 to 2
30 minutes

𝓜ain 𝓜eals
𝓜exican 𝓢tyle

Medium Saucepan with Lid

Large Skillet

Stovetop,
Microwave, or 350° Oven

INGREDIENTS:
- 1 8-oz. can VEGETARIAN REFRIED BEANS
- ¼ cup SALSA
- 1 tablespoon VEGETABLE OIL
- ½ *each* GREEN BELL PEPPERS and RED or YELLOW BELL PEPPER, seeded and sliced lengthwise (or use frozen sliced peppers)
- ½ ONION, sliced
- 3 FLOUR TORTILLAS

DIRECTIONS:
1. In saucepan, on medium-low heat, combine beans and salsa. Cover and cook until beans start to bubble. Turn heat to lowest setting, cover pan, and stir occasionally to keep beans from burning.
2. In skillet, on medium-high heat, heat vegetable oil 1 minute. Add peppers and onion. Cook and stir 5 minutes.
3. Warm tortillas in microwave 30 seconds on HIGH *or* in 350° oven for 2 minutes. Spread a thin layer of hot beans in the middle of each tortilla. Add bell pepper mixture, roll up, and enjoy.

INGREDIENTS:

- 1 box MACARONI and CHEESE MIX
- 1 15-oz. can CRUSHED TOMATOES, drained
- 1 8-oz. can VEGETARIAN BEANS
- couple plops BARBECUE SAUCE
- 2 tablespoons CHILI or TACO SEASONING

DIRECTIONS:

1. In large saucepan, cook macaroni and cheese according to package directions (about 15 minutes).
2. Stir in tomatoes, beans, barbecue sauce, and seasoning. Turn heat to medium, stir, and cook for about 5 minutes, or until heated through.

Serve with Coleslaw with Sweet & Creamy Dressing (page 22).

Tex-Mex Macaroni Surprise

Serves 2
20 minutes

*Main Meals
Mexican Style*

Large Saucepan
Stovetop

Tortilla Casserole

Serves 1 to 2
35 minutes

Main Meals
Mexican Style

8" x 8" Baking Dish (rubbed
lightly with cooking oil or
nonstick cooking spray)

350° Oven

INGREDIENTS:
- 4 FLOUR TORTILLAS, torn into 2" pieces
- 1 8-oz. can CORN KERNELS
- 1 4-oz. can DICED GREEN CHILIES
- couple handfuls shredded CHEDDAR CHEESE
- 1 15-oz. can VEGETARIAN CHILI

DIRECTIONS:
Preheat oven to 350°.
1. In baking dish, layer half of tortilla pieces, corn, chilies, one handful cheese, and the rest of the tortilla pieces.
2. Spoon chili over tortillas and top with remaining cheese.
3. Bake for 30 minutes, or until cheese is bubbly and hot.

INGREDIENTS:
- 1 tablespoon OLIVE OIL
- 1 GARLIC CLOVE, cut into tiny pieces (see tip, page 123)
- 1 medium ZUCCHINI, cut into thin strips lengthwise
- ½ BELL PEPPER, seeded and cut into thin strips lengthwise
- couple shakes CHILI POWDER
- 4 FLOUR TORTILLAS
- 1 15-oz. can ENCHILADA SAUCE
- 1 cup grated MONTEREY JACK or CHEDDAR CHEESE

DIRECTIONS:
1. In skillet, on high heat, heat olive oil 1 minute. Add garlic, zucchini, bell pepper, and chili powder. Cook 4 minutes, or until vegetables are lightly browned.
2. Lay tortillas flat and spread vegetables on one side, then roll up.
3. In oiled baking dish, lay tortillas side by side. Pour enchilada sauce over evenly and top with cheese. Bake at 350° for 20 minutes, or until cheese is bubbly.

Zucchini Enchiladas

Serves 1 to 2
30 minutes

Main Meals
Mexican Style

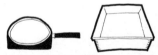

Skillet, 8" x 8" Baking Dish
(rubbed lightly with
vegetable oil)

Stovetop, 350° Oven

Microwave Meals in Minutes

SCRAMBLED EGGS:

In large microwave-safe cup scramble with fork:
- 2 EGGS

Cover tightly with plastic wrap. Microwave at 70% for 1 ½ minutes. Spoon onto plate and sprinkle with salt and pepper to taste.

POACHED EGGS:

In large microwave-safe cup place:
- ¼ cup WATER
- drop vinegar

Gently crack and slip into water:
- 1 EGG (pierce egg yolk once)

Cover tightly with plastic wrap. Microwave on HIGH for 1 minute. Lift egg out gently, place in small bowl or cup, and season with salt and pepper to taste.

Another delicious way to have a poached egg is on toast.

Tips:
- Never microwave eggs in their shells; they will explode.
- Always pierce the egg yolk as it can explode while cooking.
- Don't overcook eggs. They should look moist at the end of cooking.

Serves 1 to 2

Microwave Meals in Minutes

4-cup Microwave-safe
Glass Measuring Cup

Acorn Squash

Serves 1
15 minutes

Microwave Meals in Minutes

Sharp Knife

INGREDIENTS:
- 1 ACORN SQUASH
- 1 tablespoon BUTTER or MARGARINE
- dash GARLIC SALT

DIRECTIONS:
1. With sharp knife, make 6 small slits around outside of squash.
2. Set in middle of microwave. Cook on HIGH for 10 minutes.
3. With a potholder or dish towel, remove squash from microwave. Let it sit for 5 minutes.
4. When cool enough to handle, cut in half crosswise and remove seeds.
5. Put butter in each half cavity, sprinkle with garlic salt, and enjoy.

Another delicious meal using cooked ACORN SQUASH: Fill microwaved cooked acorn squash cavity with cottage cheese, add cooked peas, top off with sunflower seeds, and sprinkle with "Lawry's" seasoned salt.

INGREDIENTS:

- ¼ cup BUTTER or MARGARINE
- ½ cup RAW CRANBERRIES
- ¼ cup BROWN SUGAR
- 2 teaspoons WATER
- ½ cup MACINTOSH APPLES, peeled, cored, and cut into ½" cubes
- 1 ACORN SQUASH, cut into 1" rings, seeds removed

DIRECTIONS:

1. In large glass 4-cup measuring cup, melt butter or margarine on HIGH 20 seconds.
2. Add cranberries, brown sugar, and water to melted butter or margarine. Stir to mix.
3. Cook on HIGH 2–3 minutes, or until cranberry skins have popped, stirring once during cooking.
4. Add apples to cranberry mixture.
5. In microwave-safe pan, lay squash rings. Spoon cranberry-apple mixture into each ring.
6. Cover with plastic wrap (poke several holes in plastic wrap to let steam escape) and cook on HIGH 5 minutes, or until squash is tender.

Acorn Squash Rings with Cranberries and Apples

Serves 1 to 2
10 minutes

Microwave Meals in Minutes

Microwave-safe:
4-cup Glass Measuring Cup
8" x 8" Baking Dish

Cheese Potatoes

Serves 1 to 2
10 minutes

Microwave-safe:
1-cup Glass Measuring Cup
Shallow Dish

INGREDIENTS:
- 1 POTATO, washed, scrubbed, and patted dry
- 1 tablespoon BUTTER or MARGARINE
- couple shakes GARLIC SALT
- handful chopped assorted FRESH HERBS (PARSLEY, BASIL, TARRAGON, or your favorites)
- handful shredded CHEDDAR CHEESE
- couple shakes GRATED PARMESAN CHEESE

DIRECTIONS:
1. Cut potato into ¼" slices but NOT all the way through (see tip*).
2. In microwave-safe measuring cup, melt butter or margarine on HIGH for 10 seconds. Stir in garlic salt and herbs.
3. In a microwave-safe dish, place potato. Pour melted butter and herbs over potato and between slices.
4. Cook on HIGH for 4 minutes.
5. Let potato sit for 5 minutes. Sprinkle with the cheeses and microwave on HIGH for another 1–2 minutes, or until cheeses are melted and potatoes are soft.

*Tip: Place potato next to a wooden spoon when you slice. The knife will not cut down through the potato when you press down.

INGREDIENTS:

- ½ cup SOFT MARGARINE
- ½ cup SUGAR
- 2 EGGS
- 1 teaspoon VANILLA FLAVORING EXTRACT
- ½ cup FLOUR (make sure flour in cup is level with ½ mark)
- 4 oz. CHOCOLATE CHIPS

DIRECTIONS:

1. In large microwave-safe bowl, stir together soft margarine and sugar until pale yellow color. Microwave at 50% power for 30 seconds.
2. Beat with large wooden spoon until creamy and smooth.
3. Stir in eggs and vanilla. Add flour and stir until smooth.
4. In small microwave-safe bowl or cup, melt chocolate chips at 50% power for 30 seconds. Stir into batter till chocolate is evenly distributed.
5. Pour into lightly oiled microwave-safe baking pan.
6. Microwave at 50% power for 10 minutes. Remove and let sit for 10 minutes. (Top will be firm; underside will be moist.)

Have with a scoop of vanilla ice cream. Yummm!

Chocolate Brownie Pudding

Serves 2 to 3
15 minutes

Microwave Meals in Minutes

Microwave-safe: Large Bowl,
Small Bowl or Cup,
8" x 8" Baking Pan (rubbed
lightly with vegetable oil)

Polenta, "What Is It?"

Serves 1 to 2
10 minutes

Microwave Meals in Minutes

Microwave-safe Bowl

INGREDIENTS:
- 1 cup VEGETABLE BROTH
- ¼ cup CORNMEAL
- ¼ teaspoon SALT

DIRECTIONS:
1. In microwave-safe bowl, combine all ingredients and stir to mix well.
2. Microwave on HIGH 3 minutes, stirring twice. (Depending on the power of your microwave, you may have to stir and microwave at 1-minute intervals for up to 3 more minutes.)
3. Let sit about 4 minutes for firm polenta.

Polenta is a great homemade corn base to be topped with the delicious recipes on the following page.

POLENTA PANCAKES (Non-Microwave, Stovetop):

- With wet hands, pat polenta into small ball and flatten. In skillet on high heat, melt 2 tablespoons margarine or butter. Place polenta into skillet and turn to brown all sides. Serve with hot maple syrup.

POLENTA DIPPERS (Non-Microwave, Stovetop):

- Cut firm polenta into thin squares. In skillet on high heat, melt 2 tablespoons margarine or butter. Place polenta into skillet and turn to brown all sides. Dip into tomato salsa.

POLENTA PIZZA (Non-Microwave, 400° Oven):

- Flatten polenta onto pizza pan, top with pizza sauce, chopped fresh garlic, cut-up fresh basil leaves, sliced fresh onions, thinly sliced green bell peppers, and sliced fresh mushrooms. Top with lots of shredded mozzarella cheese. Bake in 400° oven 8 minutes, or until hot and bubbly.

POLENTA & CHILI (Non-Microwave, 350° Oven):

- Spread polenta over bottom of lightly oiled 8" x 8" baking dish. Top with 1 can vegetarian chili. Sprinkle with shredded cheese. Cover with foil and bake in 350° oven for 20 minutes.

Polenta, "What to Do with It?"

Several servings

Microwave Meals in Minutes

Popeye's Platter

Serves 1 to 2
15 minutes

*Microwave Meals
in Minutes*

Microwave-safe:
Medium Mixing Bowl
Casserole with Lid

INGREDIENTS:
- ½ cup WATER
- ½ cup INSTANT BROWN RICE
- 4 cups FRESH SPINACH LEAVES
- 1 CARROT, shredded
- 3 whole GREEN ONIONS, sliced
- 1 tablespoon MARGARINE or BUTTER
- 1 EGG, lightly beaten with fork in cup
- handful shredded CHEDDAR CHEESE
- couple sprinkles GARLIC SALT

DIRECTIONS:
1. In medium mixing bowl, add water and microwave at HIGH 2 minutes, or until boiling. Stir in rice and set aside.
2. In casserole dish, combine spinach, carrot, onions, and margarine. Cover and microwave on HIGH 4 minutes.
3. Mix in rice, egg, cheese, and garlic salt and stir. Microwave on HIGH, uncovered, 5 minutes, or until center is set. (It is set when butter knife inserted in center comes out clean.)

INGREDIENTS:
- 1 8-oz. can PINTO BEANS, drained well
- 1 TOMATO, chopped
- 1 GREEN ONION, sliced (green ends included)
- couple handfuls shredded CHEDDAR CHEESE
- TORTILLA CHIPS

DIRECTIONS:
1. Dump beans into microwave-safe bowl.
2. Top with tomato, onion, and cheese.
3. Cover lightly with paper towel.
4. Microwave on HIGH for 2 minutes.
5. Sprinkle with crunched-up tortilla chips.

Tastes great with topped homemade salsa and sour cream.

To freshen stale crackers or chips, lay chips or crackers between paper towels and microwave on HIGH 30 seconds.

Quick Pinto Bean Supper

Serves 1
5 minutes

Microwave Meals in Minutes

Microwave-safe Bowl

Simple Sauces

Each recipe makes about 1 cup
5 minutes

4-cup Microwave-safe
Glass Measuring Cup

BASIC WHITE SAUCE:

In large microwave-safe glass measuring cup, microwave 2 tablespoons margarine or butter at HIGH 30 seconds.

Remove from microwave and gradually stir in 2 tablespoons flour and 1 cup milk.

Microwave at HIGH for 2 minutes. Stir and microwave at HIGH additional 2 minutes, or until sauce thickens.

CHEESE SAUCE:

Stir in 1 cup shredded Cheddar cheese before last 2 minutes of microwaving.

SOUPER SAUCE:

In large microwave-safe glass bowl, stir together contents of 1 can creamed soup (mushroom, celery, tomato, etc.) and ½ cup liquid (use milk, vegetable broth, tomato juice, etc.).

Microwave at HIGH for 3–6 minutes (depending on soup used), or until smooth and heated through.

Remove and stir every 2 minutes to check on temperature and texture.

BROWN MUSHROOM SAUCE:

In large microwave-safe glass measuring cup, put 3 fresh mushrooms, thinly
    sliced, and 2 tablespoons butter or margarine.

Microwave at HIGH 1 minute.

Remove from microwave and gradually stir in 2 tablespoons flour.

Microwave at HIGH 1 minute. Gradually stir in 1 cup whole milk or light
    cream (not sour cream).

Microwave at HIGH for 2 minutes. Stir and microwave at HIGH another 2
    minutes. Stir.

PROCESSED CHEESE SAUCE:

Remove lid from glass jar and microwave at 60% 1 minute. Stir and use.
Recap and refrigerate remaining cheese.

Tips:
- Use containers that are twice the height of the sauce inside. This prevents sauce from boiling over.
- Don't overstir sauces. It only takes a couple stirs to distribute heat and get the consistency you want.

More Simple Sauces

Each recipe makes 1 cup sauce

*Microwave Meals
in Minutes*

4-cup Microwave-safe
Glass Measuring Cup

Pasta & Italian Dishes

INGREDIENTS:

- 2 tablespoons OLIVE OIL
- 3 GARLIC CLOVES, chopped
- 6 fresh MUSHROOMS, sliced
- 4 ROMA TOMATOES, chopped into ¼" pieces
- 6 large FRESH BASIL LEAVES, cut up
- dash SALT & PEPPER, to taste
- 8 oz. ANGEL HAIR PASTA

DIRECTIONS:

In large saucepan add water to ¾ full. Heat on high heat to boiling while preparing sauce:

1. In skillet, over high heat, heat oil 1 minute. Stir in garlic and mushrooms. Cook and stir a couple of minutes, or until mushrooms are soft.
2. Reduce heat to medium, add tomatoes, basil leaves, and salt and pepper and stir to blend ingredients well. Cook 6 minutes, stirring occasionally.

While sauce cooks:

1. Add angel hair pasta to the boiling water in saucepan and cook according to package directions. Watch time carefully: *Angel hair pasta cooks very quickly!*
2. Drain cooked pasta well.

Angel Hair Pasta with Fresh Tomatoes

Serves 2
15 minutes

*Pasta &
Italian Dishes*

Large Saucepan

Skillet

Stovetop

Breadstick Pizza

Serves 2 to 4
40 minutes

Pasta &
Italian Dishes

Small Mixing Bowl

8" x 8" Baking Pan (rub lightly
inside pan with olive oil)

350° Oven

INGREDIENTS:

- ¼ cup OLIVE OIL
- 1 teaspoon GARLIC POWDER or 2 fresh GARLIC CLOVES, finely chopped
- 1 tablespoon DRIED OREGANO or ITALIAN HERB SEASONING
- 1 can refrigerator BREADSTICK DOUGH, cut into 2" chunks
- ½ cup grated MOZZARELLA CHEESE
- ¼ cup PIZZA SAUCE

DIRECTIONS:

1. In small bowl, pour olive oil. Stir in garlic and oregano or Italian herb seasoning.
2. Roll breadstick dough pieces in seasoned oil.
3. In the bottom of baking pan, lay one third of bread dough chunks.
4. Top with layer of half the cheese, then half the pizza sauce.
5. Repeat Steps 3 and 4, ending with a layer of bread dough.
6. Bake at 350° for 30 minutes, or until brown.

INGREDIENTS:

- 8 oz. FETTUCCINE, cooked according to package directions
- 2 tablespoons OLIVE OIL
- 1 fresh GARLIC CLOVE, chopped
- 12 fresh MUSHROOMS, sliced
- ¼ ONION, chopped
- 1 cup FRESH SPINACH, washed, dried, and torn into pieces
- 2 tablespoons VEGETABLE BROTH or WATER
- 1 ½ cups RICOTTA CHEESE
- ½ cup GRATED ROMANO or PARMESAN CHEESE
- ¼ cup MILK
- ¼ teaspoon BLACK PEPPER

DIRECTIONS:

While pasta is cooking, make the sauce as follows:

1. In skillet, heat oil on high heat 1 minute. Add garlic, mushrooms, and onion and stir. Cook for 2 minutes.
2. Turn heat to medium and add spinach and vegetable broth. Bring to a boil and cook 5 minutes.
3. In large serving bowl, combine ricotta cheese, Romano cheese, milk, and pepper. Add hot spinach mushroom mixture and hot drained fettuccine. Toss well to mix and enjoy!

Serves 1 to 2
15 minutes

Pasta & Italian Dishes

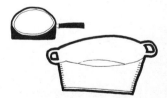

Skillet, Large Serving Bowl

Stovetop

Fried Spaghetti

Serves 1 to 2
15 minutes

Pasta &
Italian Dishes

Large Saucepan

Large Skillet

Stovetop

INGREDIENTS:
- 4 oz. SPAGHETTI, cooked according to package directions
- 2 tablespoons VEGETABLE OIL
- ½ RED ONION, cut into ½" pieces
- 2 GARLIC CLOVES, cut into very small pieces
- pinch ITALIAN HERB SEASONING
- 1 tablespoon TOMATO PASTE
- couple dashes each SALT & PEPPER

DIRECTIONS:
While the spaghetti is cooking:
1. In skillet, over medium heat, heat oil 1 minute. Add onion, garlic, and Italian seasoning. Stir and cook 2 minutes.
2. Add tomato paste and salt and pepper. Stir well and cook for 3 minutes.
3. Add the freshly cooked and well-drained spaghetti to the sauce, stirring to coat spaghetti with the tomato mixture.
4. Lower heat to medium, cover pan, and cook 3–5 minutes.
5. Stir well and eat right out of the pan.

Dip hot garlic bread into sauce as you gobble up the pasta. Yummm!

INGREDIENTS:

- 4 oz. LINGUINE, cooked according to package directions
- 2 tablespoons OLIVE OIL
- 1 tablespoon MARGARINE
- 2 fresh GARLIC CLOVES, cut into tiny pieces (see tip, page 123)
- ¼ teaspoon each DRIED TARRAGON and BASIL (if fresh is available, use 1 teaspoon of each)
- 1 small ZUCCHINI, cut into ½" cubes
- 1 GREEN ONION, thinly sliced
- handful FROZEN PEAS
- dash BLACK PEPPER
- 2 tablespoons GRATED ROMANO CHEESE

DIRECTIONS:

While linguine is cooking:

1. In a large skillet, on medium-high heat, heat olive oil and margarine 1 minute. Stir in garlic and herbs and cook 2 minutes. Reduce heat to medium.
2. Toss in zucchini and green onion and cook for 3 minutes. Add frozen peas. Cook 2 more minutes.
3. Add the cooked, drained linguine and toss to mix evenly.
4. Add pepper and sprinkle with grated Romano cheese. Heat 1 minute and serve.

Linguine with Vegetables and Herbs

Serves 1 to 2
20 minutes

Pasta & Italian Dishes

Large Skillet
Large Saucepan
Stovetop

Lynn's Tofu Spinach Lasagne

Serves 2 to 3
50 minutes

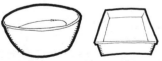

Large Mixing Bowl

8" x 8" Baking Pan (rub inside pan lightly with cooking oil or use nonstick cooking spray)

350° Oven

INGREDIENTS:
- 6 oz. FIRM TOFU, drained and blotted dry on paper towels
- 2 EGGS
- handful shredded MOZZARELLA CHEESE
- couple spoonfuls GRATED PARMESAN CHEESE (save some extra cheese for the topping)
- 1 10-oz. pkg. FROZEN CHOPPED SPINACH, defrosted and squeezed dry (use your hands to squeeze out excess water)
- 1 8-oz. package NO-BOIL LASAGNE
- 1 26-oz. jar SPAGHETTI or PASTA SAUCE (your choice)

DIRECTIONS:
1. In large bowl, crumble the tofu.
2. Add eggs and beat lightly with a fork. Dump in cheeses and spinach. Mix well.
3. In baking pan, layer all ingredients, starting with thin layer of sauce and ending with sauce on top. Sprinkle with the extra Parmesan cheese.
4. Bake in 350° oven for 25 minutes, or until lasagne is browned and bubbly.

You'll use this recipe over and over! It's good and it's easy!

INGREDIENTS:

- 2 tablespoons OLIVE or VEGETABLE OIL
- 2 fresh GARLIC CLOVES, cut into tiny pieces
- ½ ONION, chopped into ½" pieces
- 2 teaspoons dried ITALIAN SEASONING
- 10 fresh MUSHROOMS, sliced
- 1 4-oz. can TOMATO PASTE + 1 can WATER
- 1 15-oz. can TOMATO SAUCE
- 1 15-oz. can PEELED CUT-UP TOMATOES
- 1 ZUCCHINI, cut into ½" slices
- 1 YELLOW CROOKNECK SQUASH, cut into ½" cubes
- 1 teaspoon SALT
- ½ teaspoon PEPPER

DIRECTIONS:

1. In skillet, on high heat, heat oil 1 minute. Add garlic, onion, and herbs. Stir and cook 3 minutes.
2. Turn heat to medium high. Stir in tomato paste, water, sauce, and cut-up tomatoes. Add zucchini, crookneck squash, mushrooms, and salt and pepper. Stir well.
3. When sauce starts to bubble, turn heat to lowest setting. Cover with lid and cook slowly at least 1 hour, stirring occasionally.

If you have time, let sauce cook slowly a couple of hours.

Mom's Best Pasta Sauce

Serves 2 to 3
1 hour

Pasta & Italian Dishes

Large Skillet with Lid
Stovetop

95

Southern-Style Pasta

Serves 1 to 2
35 minutes

Pasta & Italian Dishes

Large Saucepan

Skillet

Stovetop

INGREDIENTS:
- 6–8 oz. PASTA, your choice, cooked according to package directions
- 2 tablespoons OLIVE or VEGETABLE OIL
- 1 BELL PEPPER, chopped
- ½ ONION, chopped
- 2 fresh GARLIC CLOVES, cut into tiny pieces (see tip, page 123)
- handful sliced MUSHROOMS
- 1 15-oz. can BLACK-EYED PEAS
- 1 10-oz. package FROZEN OKRA
- ½ 27-oz. jar PASTA SAUCE, your choice

DIRECTIONS:
While pasta is cooking, make the sauce as follows:
1. In a large skillet, on high heat, heat oil 1 minute. Stir in pepper, onion, garlic, and mushrooms. Cook 3 minutes.
2. Add black-eyed peas, okra, and pasta sauce. Stir. Turn heat to low, cover, and cook 30 minutes.
3. Serve over drained hot pasta.

INGREDIENTS:
- 1 small SPAGHETTI SQUASH, cut in half lengthwise, remove and discard seeds
- couple handfuls shredded SWISS CHEESE
- couple handfuls shredded MOZZARELLA CHEESE
- ½ 27-oz. jar SPAGHETTI SAUCE
- sprinkling GRATED PARMESAN CHEESE

DIRECTIONS:

Preheat oven to 350°.
1. Fill saucepan with 2 inches of water. On high heat, bring water just to boil. Reduce heat to medium.
2. Place squash halves, cut sides down, in water. Cover and cook 15 minutes. Remove squash and cool 5 minutes.
3. Holding each squash half with a potholder, run a fork across the pulp and put spaghetti squash strands into large bowl. (Set squash halves to side to use later as "serving bowls.")
4. Add to the large bowl with the spaghetti squash strands, Swiss cheese, mozzarella cheese, and spaghetti sauce. Toss gently until mixed well.
5. Scoop the mixture back into squash shells, top with Parmesan, and bake at 350° for 25 minutes.

"Spaghetti Squash?"

Serves 2
45 minutes

*Pasta &
Italian Dishes*

Large Saucepan
Large Mixing Bowl
Stovetop
350° Oven

Totally Easy Pasta Pesto Sauce

Makes about 1 cup sauce

Pasta & Italian Dishes

Blender

Stovetop

INGREDIENTS:

- 8 oz. PASTA (your choice), cooked according to package directions
- ¾ cup FRESH BASIL LEAVES (packed firmly in cup)
- ¼ cup PINE NUTS or WALNUTS
- 2 GARLIC CLOVES, peeled
- ⅓ cup OLIVE OIL
- ½ cup GRATED PARMESAN CHEESE
- dash SALT & PEPPER

DIRECTIONS:

While pasta cooks, prepare the pesto sauce:

1. In blender jar, place basil, nuts, and garlic cloves. Blend on high speed until finely chopped. (Stop blender several times and stir with long-handled wooden spoon to get even consistency.)
2. With blender running on medium speed, slowly pour in olive oil.
3. Add cheese and salt and pepper. Blend just to mix well. (If you like it thinner, blend in a spoonful hot water.)
4. Toss lightly with drained hot pasta.

This recipe keeps well in the refrigerator for a couple weeks.

INGREDIENTS:

- 2 ZUCCHINI, thinly sliced
- ½ ONION, thinly sliced
- 1 14-oz. jar PASTA SAUCE with MUSHROOMS
- 8 oz. sliced or shredded PROVOLONE CHEESE
- ¼ cup shredded or grated PARMESAN CHEESE
- ¼ cup packaged BREAD CRUMBS
- dash ITALIAN SEASONING
- dash GARLIC SALT
- 2 tablespoons BUTTER, melted

DIRECTIONS:

Preheat oven to 350°.

1. In baking dish, lay half of zucchini slices. Top with half of sliced onion and 1 cup of sauce. Layer with half of cheese, sprinkle half of bread crumbs over, and add half of seasonings.
2. Repeat Step 1.
3. Drizzle melted butter over bread crumb topping.
4. Bake in 350° oven for 1 hour, or until top is brown and crusty.

Zucchini Parmesana

Serves 2 to 3
70 minutes

*Pasta &
Italian Dishes*

8" x 8" Baking Dish
(rubbed with vegetable oil to
prevent sticking)
350° Oven

Beans & Rice Dishes

INGREDIENTS:
- 2 cups BROWN RICE, cooked according to package directions (or use reheated LEFTOVER RICE)
- 1 tablespoon OLIVE OIL
- ½ ONION, chopped
- 1 15-oz. can CUT-UP TOMATOES
- 1 15-oz. can KIDNEY BEANS, drained
- 1 8-oz. can CORN KERNELS, drained
- CHILI POWDER, if you like it spicy (optional)
- dash SALT & PEPPER

DIRECTIONS:
While rice cooks:
1. In skillet on high heat, heat olive oil 1 minute. Add onion and cook 2 minutes.
2. Add tomatoes, beans, and corn. Stir and cook for 5 minutes.
3. Turn heat to lowest setting. Add spices and cook for 20 minutes.
4. Serve over hot rice.

Beans and Corn on Rice

Serves 2
30 minutes

Beans & Rice Dishes

Skillet
Stovetop

Caribbean Red Beans and Rice

Serves 2
35 minutes

Beans & Rice Dishes

Large Saucepan

Stovetop

INGREDIENTS:

- 1 tablespoon OLIVE OIL
- 1 ONION, chopped into ¼" pieces
- 2 GARLIC CLOVES, chopped into small pieces (see tip, page 123)
- ¼ teaspoon each: GROUND NUTMEG, CINNAMON, and GROUND CLOVES
- SALT & PEPPER to taste
- 1 8-oz. can KIDNEY BEANS (drain and save liquid)
- 1 14-oz. can CUT-UP TOMATOES (drain and save liquid)
- ½ cup RAW RICE (*not* instant)

DIRECTIONS:

1. In saucepan, on medium-high heat, heat oil and add onion and garlic. Cook for 3 minutes, or until onion is limp. Add spices and stir to blend flavors. Lower heat to medium.
2. Add beans and tomatoes. Stir and cook for 5 minutes.
3. In measuring cup, combine reserved liquids from beans and tomatoes, adding water to equal 1 cup. Set aside.
4. Stir rice into bean mixture and add 1 cup liquid from Step 3.
5. On high heat, bring mixture to a boil. Immediately, turn heat to lowest setting, cover, and cook slowly, about 25 minutes, or until the rice is firm but tender.

INGREDIENTS:

- ¼ cup BUTTER or MARGARINE
- ½ small ONION, chopped
- 2 stalks CELERY, chopped
- 1 cup LONG-GRAIN BROWN RICE (*not* instant)
- 1 package DRY VEGETABLE SOUP MIX
- 2 ½ cups WATER
- couple FRESH PARSLEY SPRIGS, cut up
- couple BASIL LEAVES, cut up

DIRECTIONS:

1. In skillet, on medium-high heat, melt butter. Add onion, celery, and rice. Cook and stir until rice is golden brown, about 5 minutes.
2. Stir in remaining ingredients. Reduce heat to low. Cover and cook 20 minutes, or until liquid is absorbed.

Garden Rice Pilaf

Serves 1 to 2
30 minutes

Beans & Rice Dishes

Skillet with Lid

Stovetop

Herbed Brown Rice

Serves 2 to 3
45 minutes

Beans & Rice Dishes

Medium Saucepan with Lid

Stovetop

INGREDIENTS:
- 1 ½ cups LONG-GRAIN BROWN RICE (*not* instant)
- ½ lb. sliced FRESH MUSHROOMS
- 1 14-oz. can VEGETABLE BROTH
- ¾ cup WATER
- 2 FRESH THYME SPRIGS (leaves only)
- 1 GREEN ONION, thinly sliced

DIRECTIONS:
1. In medium saucepan, combine rice, mushrooms, broth, and water.
2. Turn heat to high. When rice mixture comes to boiling point, turn heat to low, cover pan, and cook slowly 40 minutes, or until liquid is absorbed.
3. Remove from heat. Stir in fresh thyme and sprinkle green onions on top.

INGREDIENTS:

- 2 tablespoons BUTTER or MARGARINE
- 2 GREEN ONIONS, thinly sliced
- 1 EGG
- 1 cup COOKED RICE*
- handful FROZEN PEAS
- 1 tablespoon SOY SAUCE

DIRECTIONS:

1. In skillet, on medium-high heat, melt butter and add onions. Cook 1 minute.
2. Crack egg into skillet. Stir and drag egg lightly with fork until egg is cooked into "strings."
3. Add rice, peas, and soy sauce.
4. Cook, stirring occasionally, 3 minutes, or until rice is browned and all ingredients are hot.

*Tip: Good recipe for leftover rice.

Quick Fried Rice

Serves 1
8 minutes

Beans & Rice Dishes

Skillet
Stovetop

Tofu Fried Rice

Serves 1 to 2
10 minutes

Beans & Rice Dishes

Saucepan with Lid

Large Skillet

Stovetop

INGREDIENTS:
- 1 cup INSTANT BROWN RICE, cooked according to package directions
- 1 tablespoon MARGARINE or BUTTER
- 1 EGG, lightly beaten
- 1 tablespoon VEGETABLE OIL
- 4 oz. FIRM TOFU, patted dry with paper towels and cut into small cubes
- 1 package frozen STIR-FRY VEGETABLES with seasonings
- sprinkle SOY SAUCE

DIRECTIONS:

While rice cooks:

1. In skillet, on medium-high heat, melt margarine or butter. Add egg and let spread to form "pancake." Cook until firm. Remove to plate and set aside. When cool, cut into small strips.
2. In skillet, on medium-high heat, heat oil 1 minute. Add tofu and stir-fry vegetables.
3. Stir in cooked rice and egg strips. Season with soy sauce.

Simply Veggies

INGREDIENTS:
- ½ lb. FRESH ASPARAGUS SPEARS
- 2 tablespoons BUTTER or MARGARINE
- 1 LEMON, cut in half
- couple spoonfuls SLIVERED ALMONDS
- SALT & PEPPER to taste

DIRECTIONS:
1. Holding the middle of asparagus spears, snap off the tough end of the stalks and discard.
2. In a nonstick skillet, on medium-high heat, melt butter. Add the asparagus spears and cook 3 minutes.
3. Turn heat to low. Cover pan and cook 2 minutes, or until the asparagus is just tender and still bright green.
4. Squeeze juice from lemon over asparagus. Add slivered almonds and salt and pepper and toss gently.

Almond Asparagus

Serves 1

Skillet with Lid

Stovetop

Baked Eggplant Slices

Serves 1
15 minutes

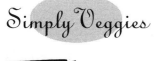

Oven Broiler Pan
(lined with aluminum foil)

Saucer or Small Plate

400° Oven

INGREDIENTS:

- 1 EGGPLANT, peeled* and cut crosswise into ½" slices
- 1 tablespoon softened BUTTER or MARGARINE
- 1 tablespoon VEGETABLE OIL
- ½ LEMON
- 1 tablespoon grated ONION (or use sprinkling DRIED ONION FLAKES)

DIRECTIONS:

Preheat oven to 400°.

1. On aluminum foil–covered cookie sheet, lay eggplant slices.
2. In a saucer or small plate, mix butter or margarine with vegetable oil. Squeeze lemon juice into butter-oil mixture and add onion.
3. Spread over both sides of eggplant slices.
4. Bake 6 minutes on one side, turn, and bake another 6 minutes, or until eggplant is tender when pierced with a fork.

Delicious dipped in catsup or chili sauce.

*Tip: To peel eggplant: cut off top and bottom of eggplant. Stand it on one end and cut peel off in downward strokes with sharp knife.

INGREDIENTS:
- 1 large RUSSET BAKING POTATO
- ¼ teaspoon VEGETABLE OIL

DIRECTIONS:
Preheat oven or toaster oven to 350°.
1. Wash and scrub potato to remove all dirt.
2. Pierce potato several times with fork.
3. Rub potato all over with vegetable oil.
4. Set in middle of preheated oven or toaster oven and bake 40 minutes, or until potato feels soft to touch.
5. Remove and wrap in clean kitchen towel to keep hot until ready to eat.

POTATO TOPPINGS & FILLINGS:
- Broccoli florets with shredded Cheddar cheese and sunflower seeds
- Hot vegetarian chili with grated Parmesan cheese
- Yogurt, ricotta cheese, or cottage cheese with soy "bacon bits"
- Cooked peas topped with Basic White Sauce (see page 84)
- Fresh Tomato Salsa (see page 130)
- Crunchy Red Slaw (see page 24)

Baked Potatoes Plus

Serves 1
45 minutes

Simply Veggies

350° Oven or Toaster Oven

Banana Squash and Carrots

Serves 1
20 minutes

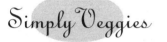

Skillet with Lid

Stovetop

INGREDIENTS:

- 1 small rectangle BANANA SQUASH, cut into 2" squares
- 12 BABY CARROTS or 2 large CARROTS, cut into 2" lengths
- 2 tablespoons BUTTER
- ½ LIME
- 4 MINT LEAVES, cut up
- SALT & PEPPER

DIRECTIONS:

1. Pour ½" water into skillet. Place squash, skin side down, in water and lay carrots on squash. Turn heat to medium high.
2. When water comes to a boil, cover pan, lower heat to medium, and cook (steam) for 20 minutes, or until squash and carrots are tender.
3. Drain pan of any excess water. Add dollops of butter onto squash and carrots. Sprinkle with lime juice and top with mint leaves. Cover pan and heat on medium low 2 minutes, until steamy hot.
4. Season to taste with salt and pepper when ready to eat.

INGREDIENTS:

- 1 head BROCCOLI, cut into small florets
- 1 LEMON, cut in quarters
- 2 tablespoons BUTTER or MARGARINE
- 2 sprigs FRESH TARRAGON LEAVES or ½ teaspoon DRIED TARRAGON
- SALT & PEPPER

DIRECTIONS:

1. In saucepan, place broccoli and add 1" of water. (Don't cover broccoli with water.) Turn heat to high and bring water to boil.
2. Cover pan and reduce heat to medium. Cook broccoli 5 minutes, or just until tender but still bright green. Drain off water.
3. Squeeze juice from lemon over broccoli. Add butter and sprinkle on tarragon.
4. Cover pan and heat for 2 minutes on medium heat. Season to taste with salt and pepper.

Broccoli with Lemon Tarragon

Serves 1
10 minutes

Small Saucepan with Lid

Stovetop

Candied Yams

Serves 1
8 minutes

Simply Veggies

Skillet

Stovetop

INGREDIENTS:

- 1 teaspoon BUTTER or MARGARINE
- 2 tablespoons WATER
- 2 tablespoons BROWN SUGAR
- ½ teaspoon GROUND CINNAMON
- ¼ teaspoon GROUND NUTMEG
- 1 15-oz. can YAMS, drained and sliced

DIRECTIONS:

1. In skillet, on medium heat, melt butter.
2. Add water, brown sugar, and spices. Heat 2 minutes, or until bubbly.
3. Add yams to pan and carefully spoon sauce over yams. Turn heat to low, cover, and heat for 5 minutes.

INGREDIENTS:

- 10 BABY CARROTS or 3 CARROTS, washed and peeled
- ½ ONION, cut into thin slices
- 1 tablespoon BUTTER or MARGARINE
- 1 large PARSLEY SPRIG, green leaves cut up
- SALT & PEPPER

DIRECTIONS:

1. In saucepan, place carrots and onion. Add water just to cover carrots. Turn heat to high and bring water to boil.
2. Cover pan with lid and turn heat down to medium.
3. Cook 8 minutes, or until carrots are just barely tender. Drain off excess water.
4. Return pan to stove. Add butter or margarine and sprinkle with parsley. Cover pan and heat on high 1 minute, or until carrots are steamy hot. Season to taste with salt and pepper.

Carrots and Onions with Parsley

Serves 1
10 minutes

Saucepan with Lid

Stovetop

Cauliflower Italiano

Serves 1
12 minutes

Simply Veggies

Skillet with Lid

Stovetop

INGREDIENTS:
- 3 tablespoons OLIVE OIL
- 1 GARLIC CLOVE, cut into tiny pieces (see tip, page 123)
- 1 small head CAULIFLOWER, washed and cut into small florets
- ½ 15-oz. can PEELED CUT-UP TOMATOES WITH HERBS
- couple sprinkles GRATED PARMESAN CHEESE

DIRECTIONS:
1. In skillet, heat oil on high 1 minute. Stir in garlic and cook 1 minute.
2. Add cauliflower. Stir and cook 3 minutes.
3. Add tomatoes (including liquid) and stir gently.
4. Reduce heat to medium low and cook for 8 minutes.
5. Sprinkle with Parmesan cheese before serving.

INGREDIENTS:

- 3 large ears fresh CORN ON COB
- 3 tablespoons VEGETABLE or OLIVE OIL
- ½ ONION, chopped
- ½ each GREEN & RED BELL PEPPER, cut into ½" pieces
- couple shakes SALT & PEPPER to taste

DIRECTIONS:

1. With a sharp knife, cut the corn kernels from the cobs.
2. In large skillet, heat oil on high heat 1 minute.
3. Add onion and peppers. Cook and stir 2 minutes.
4. Stir in corn kernels and salt and pepper and cook 5 minutes, or until heated through.

Fresh Corn and Peppers Sauté

Serves 1
7 minutes

Simply Veggies

Large Skillet
Stovetop

Fresh Vegetables with Lemon Butter

Serves 1
10 minutes

Simply Veggies

Saucepan with Lid

Stovetop

VEGETABLES:
- 1 stalk BROCCOLI, cut into florets
- 12 BABY CARROTS
- 12 GREEN BEANS, tips pinched off
- ½ head CAULIFLOWER, cut into florets
- 1 CROOKNECK or ZUCCHINI SQUASH, sliced

LEMON BUTTER:
- ½ LEMON
- 2 tablespoons BUTTER or MARGARINE
- dash SALT & PEPPER
- pinch each DRIED HERBS (e.g., marjoram, thyme, tarragon)

DIRECTIONS:
1. In saucepan, on high heat, add water to ½". Bring water to boiling. Add vegetables, cover pan, and cook 5–7 minutes, or until veggies are crispy tender. Drain pan.
2. Squeeze juice from lemon over vegetables. Add butter or margarine, salt and pepper, and herbs.
3. Turn heat to medium high. Cover pan and heat vegetables in lemon butter 1 minute or until hot and sizzling.

INGREDIENTS:

- handful ASPARAGUS SPEARS, washed and cut into 2" lengths
- 1 ZUCCHINI, quartered lengthwise and sliced into 2" lengths
- 1 cup BOILING WATER
- 1 tablespoon OLIVE OIL
- couple splashes SOY SAUCE
- squirt BALSAMIC VINEGAR (or wine vinegar)
- handful SESAME SEEDS, CASHEWS, or PINE NUTS
- BLACK PEPPER to taste

DIRECTIONS:

1. In large skillet, place asparagus and zucchini. Pour boiling water over to cover. Let sit for 3 minutes.
2. Drain water off vegetables. Return pan to stove. Turn heat to high, evaporating excess water. Add olive oil and stir-fry vegetables for 4 minutes (watch for spattering).
3. Add soy sauce, vinegar, nuts, and pepper. Cook and stir 2 minutes.

Tastes great over hot steamed rice.

Stir-Fry Asparagus and Zucchini

Serves 1 to 2
10 minutes

Simply Veggies

Large Skillet
Stovetop

"Hints & Tips"
for Vegetable Preparation
Bell Peppers

TIPS: Buy in season and freeze for use later. Watch for seasonal special prices on the more expensive red and yellow bell peppers. Buy several and freeze what you can't use now.

HOW TO FREEZE:

Remove crown, stem, and seeds. Place in individual plastic bags and seal tightly. Freeze and use later as needed. Bell peppers do not stay crisp and firm after being frozen, but they retain their nutrition and are perfect for cooking. Just slice or cut up while peppers are still frozen and add to the recipe you are making.

HOW TO CUT:

With a sharp knife, cut a circle around the crown of bell pepper.

Grab hold of stem and twist off.

Remove white membrane and seeds.

Slice in thin strips lengthwise or chop strips into small pieces (as directed by recipe).

HOW TO PEEL GARLIC:

Separate cloves from fresh garlic bulb by placing the flat blade of a large knife over garlic bulb and giving it a "whack" with the palm of your hand. Be careful and don't curve your hand down over the blade. Another simple and safe way is to give the garlic bulb a "whack" with a wooden kitchen mallet or similar heavy object. Peel off skins from each clove needed.

HOW TO MINCE GARLIC:

After skin is removed, cut off edge where root was attached and discard. Slice garlic lengthwise and chop crosswise until garlic is in small slivers or tiny pieces.

HOW TO KEEP GARLIC:

Fresh garlic bulbs keep well for many weeks if kept in a cool, dry area. Once you have opened the garlic bulb, try to use the rest of the garlic within several days as garlic tends to lose some of its sharp flavor. Store partially used garlic bulbs in vegetable bin in refrigerator.

"Hints & Tips"
for Vegetable Preparation

Lettuce

CLEANING LETTUCE:

Head Lettuce: Remove core by tapping it sharply on hard surface. Core will come out easily. Wash by holding lettuce upside down under cold running water. Turn right side up on a clean towel and let lettuce drain well.

Leaf Lettuce: Fill sink with cold water. Twist off stem and let leaves float in water. Dirt will fall to bottom of sink. Lift leaves out and drain on paper towels a few minutes.

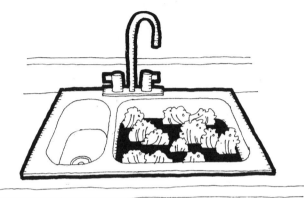

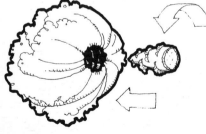

STORING LETTUCE:

Wrap washed lettuce leaves in clean kitchen towel and place towel in plastic bag. Place in refrigerator vegetable bin. Lettuce will stay fresh and crisp for about a week in refrigerator.

"Hints & Tips"
for Vegetable Preparation

Onions

ONION ODORS:

A quick way to remove onion odors from your hands is by rubbing them with celery tops.

3 EZ STEPS TO CHOPPING ONIONS:

1. Slice onion in half crosswise. Remove and discard outer onion skin.

2. Holding each onion half with cut side down, slice in 4 slices.

3. Holding onion together, slice crosswise to the prior cuts, making cuts close together for small pieces of chopped onion.

Quick Salsas & Sauces

Cucumber Raita

Makes 1 cup
10 minutes

Small Bowl with Lid

INGREDIENTS:
- 1 CUCUMBER, peeled
- 1 8-oz. container PLAIN YOGURT
- 1 tablespoon SOFT CREAM CHEESE
- 2 GARLIC CLOVES, cut into very small pieces
- squirt HOT SAUCE (e.g., "Tabasco")
- juice from ½ LEMON
- 1 GREEN ONION, thinly sliced (green parts included)
- dash BLACK PEPPER

DIRECTIONS:
1. To prepare cucumber, cut in half lengthwise and scoop out seeds. Chop rest of cucumber into very small pieces and place in mixing bowl.
2. Add rest of ingredients and stir to mix well.
3. Cover and refrigerate until ready to use.

Tastes fabulous dipped with warm pita bread.

INGREDIENTS:
- 1 cup SOUR CREAM
- ½ cup MAYONNAISE
- 1 teaspoon chopped FRESH PARSLEY
- 2 teaspoons CURRY POWDER
- juice from ½ LEMON
- splash WORCESTERSHIRE SAUCE
- dash SALT

DIRECTIONS:
1. In mixing bowl, combine all ingredients. Stir to mix well.
2. Cover and refrigerate until ready to use.

Delicious with hot or cold vegetables as a sauce or a dip.

Curry Dipping Sauce

Makes 2 cups
10 minutes

Quick Salsas & Sauces

Small Bowl with Lid

Fresh Tomato Salsa

Makes 1 cup
10 minutes

Quick Salsas & Sauces

Small Bowl with Lid

INGREDIENTS:
- 1 small RED ONION, chopped
- 2 TOMATOES, chopped
- handful CILANTRO, cut up (amount used depends on taste)
- ½ GREEN BELL PEPPER, chopped
- juice from ½ LIME
- splash HOT SAUCE (e.g., "Tabasco")

DIRECTIONS:
1. In small bowl, combine all ingredients.
2. Stir to mix well.
3. Cover and refrigerate any remaining salsa. Keeps fresh for a couple of days.

There are a million uses for this simple salsa: as a topping for pasta to dips for hot nachos to spicy additions to soups.

INGREDIENTS:
- 1 6-oz. container VANILLA YOGURT
- handful FLAKED COCONUT
- 1 8-oz. can CRUSHED PINEAPPLE, drained well*
- 1 tablespoon BROWN SUGAR

DIRECTIONS:
1. In small bowl, stir all ingredients together well to blend flavors.
2. Cover and refrigerate until ready to use.

Serving Ideas:
- Use over cake cubes for a delicious dessert.
- Use as a dip with cheese for party appetizers.
- Use as a dressing for fresh fruit salad.

*Tip: When draining pineapple, push down on pineapple to squeeze out extra juices and drain into glass. Makes a great juice to drink or add to fruit smoothies.

Fruit and Yogurt Sauce

Makes 1 cup
5 minutes

Quick Salsas & Sauces

Small Bowl with Lid

Hot Mustard Sauce

Makes ½ cup
10 minutes

*Quick Salsas
& Sauces*

Small Saucepan

Stovetop

INGREDIENTS:
- 1 tablespoon BUTTER or MARGARINE
- ½ ONION, chopped
- ¼ cup PREPARED MUSTARD
- ¼ cup WHOLE MILK or CREAM
- 1 teaspoon WORCESTERSHIRE SAUCE
- dash SALT & PEPPER

DIRECTIONS:
1. In saucepan, on medium heat, melt butter or margarine. Add onion. Stir and cook for 1 minute, or until onion is soft.
2. Stir in the mustard and cream (or milk), stirring until heated and steam rises. (Don't let sauce boil or it will burn.)
3. Stir in Worcestershire sauce and salt and pepper. Serve while hot.

INGREDIENTS:
- 1 15-oz. can GARBANZO BEANS, drained
- 3 tablespoons LEMON JUICE
- ¼ cup TAHINI SESAME PASTE (or make your own with 1/4 cup toasted sesame seeds mixed with 2 tablespoons olive oil)
- ¼ teaspoon ground CUMIN
- 2 GARLIC CLOVES, cut into thirds

DIRECTIONS:
1. Place all ingredients in the blender and cover.
2. Blend on high until smooth and heavy in consistency.

Delicious served with Toasted Pita Bread:
Toast pita bread in a toaster oven or oven until golden.
Tear hot pita bread into large chunks.
Spread with hummus and enjoy!

Hummus

Makes 4 cups
5 minutes

Quick Salsas & Sauces

Blender

133

Lemon Butter & Herb Sauce

Makes ½ cup
5 minutes

Quick Salsas & Sauces

Small Saucepan

Stovetop

INGREDIENTS:
- 2 tablespoons BUTTER or MARGARINE
- 2 GREEN ONIONS, thinly sliced
- ¼ cup PARSLEY, chopped
- 3 FRESH BASIL LEAVES, cut up
- juice of ½ LEMON
- dash SALT

DIRECTIONS:
1. In small saucepan, on medium heat, heat butter or margarine 1 minute. Add onions. Stir and cook 1 minute.
2. Add parsley, basil, and lemon juice.
3. Cover pan and let sauce steam for a couple of minutes. Add salt to taste.

Pour over hot cooked vegetables or pasta.

INGREDIENTS:

- 1 TOMATO, chopped
- 1 MANGO, cut into sections, peeled, and chopped* (*The mango seed is long and thin. Cut mango lengthwise into 3 sections, leaving the inside sections about ¾" thick, with the outside sections thicker. Cut up outer third sections.*)
- 1 KIWI, peeled, pitted, and chopped
- 1 PAPAYA, peeled, seeded, and chopped
- 1 8-oz. can CRUSHED PINEAPPLE, drained
- handful SHREDDED COCONUT
- 6 FRESH MINT LEAVES, cut up
- juice of 2 LIMES
- splash "TABASCO" SAUCE

DIRECTIONS:

1. In mixing bowl, combine all ingredients.
2. Stir well to mix.
3. Cover and refrigerate until ready to use. Tastes best when used right away.

*Tip: If mango and papaya are not available, use peaches, nectarines, and melon.

Nannette's Mango & Fruit Salsa

Makes 2 cups
10 minutes

Quick Salsas & Sauces

Bowl with Lid

Olive Tapenade

Makes 2 cups
10 minutes

INGREDIENTS:
- 3 large GARLIC CLOVES, cut into tiny pieces
- ½ cup PIMENTO-STUFFED GREEN OLIVES, finely chopped
- ½ cup PITTED BLACK OLIVES, finely chopped
- ¼ cup ROASTED SWEET RED PEPPERS, cut into small bite-size pieces
- ¼ cup OLIVE OIL

DIRECTIONS:
1. In medium bowl, dump all ingredients and mix well to blend.
2. Cover and refrigerate until ready to use.

*To serve, spread on warm Italian bread chunks or use as a
condiment for veggie sandwiches.*

Medium Bowl with Lid

GLORIFIED LIMA BEANS:
Gently stir 1 cup sour cream into 2 cups hot cooked lima beans. Add 1 green onion, thinly sliced, and 1 tablespoon butter. Season as you like.

SOUR CREAM SCRAMBLE:
Gently stir 2 spoonfuls sour cream into 2 cooked soft-scrambled eggs. Top with salsa.

VEGETABLE CHEESE SAUCE:
In small saucepan, on low heat, blend 1 cup sour cream with 1 cup shredded cheddar cheese, stirring constantly. Stir in juice of ½ lemon and pour over steamed vegetables.

FRUIT TOPPER:
Blend ½ cup sour cream with 2 tablespoons brown sugar. Use as dip for fresh strawberries.

"SOUPER" SAUCE:
In saucepan, over low heat, blend 1 can condensed cream of mushroom soup with ½ cup sour cream. Heat through and pour over vegetables, rice, or eggs.

PUMPKIN PIE TOPPING:
Blend ⅓ cup toasted flaked coconut with ¼ cup sour cream.

Simply Sour Cream

Several servings

Quick Salsas
& Sauces

Spicy Avocado Dip

Makes 1 cup
5 minutes

Quick Salsas
& Sauces

Small Bowl with Lid

INGREDIENTS:
- 1 AVOCADO, peeled and pitted (keep seed to use later)*
- 1 whole GREEN ONION, thinly sliced
- 1 GARLIC CLOVE, chopped into very small pieces
- 1 LEMON, cut in half
- 1 tablespoon SALSA (mild to spicy, your choice)
- 2 tablespoons SOUR CREAM

DIRECTIONS:
1. In small mixing bowl, cut avocado into small pieces and mash with fork.
2. Add onion, garlic, and lemon juice. Stir well to blend flavors.
3. Add salsa and sour cream. Blend with fork until creamy and pale green in color.

*Tip: If not going to use avocado dip right away, place the avocado seed into middle of dip to keep the dip from turning brown. Cover bowl and refrigerate. Keeps for 1–2 days.

INGREDIENTS:

- 1 tablespoon SOY SAUCE
- 2 tablespoons SUGAR
- 4 teaspoons GROUND GINGER
- 1 GARLIC CLOVE, chopped into tiny pieces
- 2 tablespoons VEGETABLE OIL
- ½ cup VEGETABLE BROTH

DIRECTIONS:

1. In small bowl or jar with lid, combine all ingredients and mix thoroughly.
2. Keep covered tightly in refrigerator until ready to use.

EXOTIC VEGETABLES

Pour teriyaki sauce over cubes of green peppers, onions, and mushrooms in a plastic bag. Let vegetables sit in marinade 15–20 minutes. Pour vegetables and sauce into a hot skillet and stir-fry for 6 minutes, but *watch for spattering!*

Best served over hot steamed rice.

Teriyaki Sauce

Makes ¾ cup
5 minutes

Quick Salsas
& Sauces

Small Bowl or Jar with Lid

Desserts & Snacks

INGREDIENTS:

- 2 tablespoons FLOUR
- 1 BANANA, sliced lengthwise into ¼" slices
- couple shakes CINNAMON SUGAR (See page 3.)
- 2 tablespoons VEGETABLE OIL

DIRECTIONS:

1. Spread flour on dinner plate. Lightly roll banana slices in flour.
2. Empty excess flour off plate and return bananas to plate. Sprinkle both sides of bananas with cinnamon sugar until heavily coated.
3. In skillet, add oil and heat on high heat for 1 minute. Add bananas and fry on both sides until lightly browned.
4. Serve topped with ice cream or frozen yogurt and sprinkled liberally with cinnamon sugar.

Banana Fritters

Serves 1
5 minutes

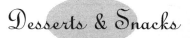

Desserts & Snacks

Skillet

Dinner Plate

Stovetop

Foolproof Rhubarb Crumble

Serves 2 to 4

Large Mixing Bowl

8" x 8" Baking Dish (rubbed lightly with cooking oil or nonstick cooking spray)

350° Oven

INGREDIENTS:

- 4 stalks RHUBARB, cut into ½" pieces
- 1 APPLE, peeled, cored, and cut into 1" cubes
- 1 cup sliced fresh or frozen STRAWBERRIES
- ⅓ cup GRANULATED SUGAR
- ½ teaspoon GROUND CINNAMON
- ½ cup FLOUR
- 1 teaspoon BAKING POWDER
- ¼ teaspoon SALT
- 4 tablespoons BUTTER or MARGARINE
- ⅔ cup BROWN SUGAR
- ⅔ cup QUICK-COOKING OATS

DIRECTIONS:

Preheat oven to 350°.

1. In baking dish, combine rhubarb, apple, and strawberries.
2. Stir together sugar and cinnamon in small cup. Sprinkle over fruit.
3. In mixing bowl, combine flour, baking powder, and salt. Add butter, mixing with fork until crumbly. Stir in brown sugar and oats. Sprinkle over cinnamon-sugared fruit.
4. Bake for 45 minutes, or until lightly browned.

Delicious with cold milk poured over the hot rhubarb.

INGREDIENTS:

- 1 large BANANA
- 1 cup CHOCOLATE CHIPS
- 1 cup chopped ROASTED PEANUTS or ALMONDS

DIRECTIONS:

1. Place the banana on aluminum foil (curve sides of foil up to catch melted chocolate).
2. In large microwave-safe bowl, dump chocolate chips and melt on HIGH for 30 seconds. Stir until smooth.
3. Immediately pour melted chocolate (sauce) over banana, rolling banana to cover completely. Sprinkle with nuts on all sides.
4. Fold foil up loosely around banana. Seal and put in freezer until ready to eat.

Frozen Chocolate-Covered Bananas

Serves 1
2 minutes plus freezing time

Desserts & Snacks

Large Microwave-safe Bowl
Aluminum Foil

Grammi's Caramel Corn

Makes enough for 1 quart of popped corn
5 minutes

Desserts & Snacks

Medium Saucepan

Microwave

Stovetop

INGREDIENTS:

- 1 package microwave POPCORN
- ½ cup BUTTER or MARGARINE
- 1 cup BROWN SUGAR
- ½ teaspoon SALT (omit if using salted popcorn)
- 2 tablespoons WATER

DIRECTIONS:

Make popcorn in microwave according to package directions.

1. In saucepan, melt butter on medium-high heat.
2. Stir in brown sugar, salt, and water. Cook 2–3 minutes, stirring constantly.
3. Immediately pour over hot popped corn and toss with wooden spoon.

INGREDIENTS:

- ½ cup WATER
- ½ cup SUGAR
- ½ teaspoon VANILLA or MAPLE FLAVORING EXTRACT
- dash SALT
- 2 MACINTOSH APPLES, peeled, cored, and cut into quarters
- scoop of VANILLA ICE CREAM or FROZEN YOGURT

DIRECTIONS:

1. In saucepan, stir together water, sugar, extract (vanilla or maple), and salt. Turn heat to high and bring mixture to boil.
2. Add apples. Turn heat to low. Cook slowly for 10 minutes, or until apples are just tender.
3. Serve in bowl and top with vanilla ice cream or frozen yogurt.

For an extra delicious treat, place a crumbled sugar cookie in bottom of bowl before adding apples. Top off with the scoop of vanilla ice cream.

Hot Apples & Ice Cream

Serves 1
12 minutes

Desserts & Snacks

Saucepan
Small Serving Bowl
Stovetop

"Just Like Mom's" Rice Pudding

Serves 2 to 3
20 minutes

Desserts & Snacks

INGREDIENTS:
- 1 ½ cups MILK
- 1 cup INSTANT RICE (uncooked)
- 1 EGG
- ¼ cup SUGAR
- dash SALT
- 1 teaspoon VANILLA FLAVORING EXTRACT

DIRECTIONS:
1. In saucepan, on medium heat, heat milk just until it starts to boil.
2. Stir in rice. Cover and remove from heat. Let stand 10 minutes.
3. In mixing bowl, beat together egg, sugar, salt, and vanilla with wooden spoon (or electric mixer, if you have one) until thick and smooth.
4. Pour into cooked rice. Cook and stir on low heat 8 minutes.

Serve warm or chill in refrigerator until ready to eat.

Medium Saucepan with Lid

Stovetop

INGREDIENTS:

- 4 EGGS
- ⅔ cup MILK
- ⅔ cup ORANGE JUICE
- 1 teaspoon GRATED ORANGE ZEST
- ⅓ cup SUGAR
- 3 slices BREAD, crust removed and bread cut into ½" cubes

DIRECTIONS:

Preheat oven to 350°.

1. In large mixing bowl, beat eggs with fork until well blended.
2. Add milk, orange juice, orange zest, and sugar and stir well to blend flavors.
3. Add bread cubes and lightly stir.
4. Pour mixture into baking dish. Bake for 30 minutes, or until pudding is done.

To test if pudding is done, insert a knife. If knife comes out clean with no pudding stuck to knife edges, it's done.

Orange Bread Pudding

Serves 1 to 2
40 minutes

Desserts & Snacks

Large Mixing Bowl

8" x 8" Baking Pan (lightly rubbed with margarine to prevent sticking)

350° Oven

Pumpkin Pudding

Serves 2 to 3
10 minutes

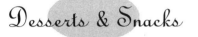

Mixing Bowl
Serving Cups

INGREDIENTS:
- 1 3-oz. package INSTANT LEMON or VANILLA PUDDING
- 2 cups cold MILK
- ½ cup canned PUMPKIN or PUMPKIN PIE FILLING
- handful SHREDDED COCONUT
- 4 GRAHAM CRACKERS, crushed
- WHIPPED CREAM DESSERT TOPPING

DIRECTIONS:
1. In mixing bowl, prepare pudding according to package instructions, using the 2 cups of cold milk.
2. Add pumpkin and coconut and stir until smooth.
3. Pour pudding into dish or cups until half full, sprinkle with crushed graham crackers, pour on remaining pudding.
4. Top with a plop of whipped topping.

Or if you can't wait, eat right out of the mixing bowl.

INGREDIENTS:

- 1 cup canned PUMPKIN
- ½ cup BISCUIT MIX (e.g., "Bisquick")
- ½ cup SUGAR
- 1 cup EVAPORATED MILK
- 1 tablespoon soft MARGARINE
- 1 ½ teaspoons PUMPKIN PIE SPICE
- 1 teaspoon VANILLA FLAVORING EXTRACT
- 2 EGGS

DIRECTIONS:

Preheat oven to 350°.

1. In blender jar, combine all ingredients.
2. Blend on medium about 2 minutes or until smooth.
3. Pour into pie plate and bake for 40 minutes, or until knife inserted in center of pie comes out clean. Cover and refrigerate any remaining pie.

This fabulous pie "magically" makes its own crust.

Rob's Amazing Pumpkin Pie

Makes 1 pie
Serves 4 to 6
45 minutes

Desserts & Snacks

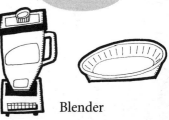

Blender
8" or 9" Pie Pan (rubbed lightly with vegetable oil)
350° Oven

Party Food

INGREDIENTS:
- 1 tablespoon VEGETABLE OIL
- 1 medium ONION, chopped
- 2 GARLIC CLOVES, minced[*]
- 1 15-oz. can REFRIED BEANS
- ¼ cup SALSA (mild or spicy, your choice)
- ¼ cup shredded CHEDDAR CHEESE

DIRECTIONS:
1. In saucepan, on high heat, heat oil and cook onion and garlic until onion is transparent, about 2–3 minutes.
2. Add beans and salsa to onion and stir well. When sauce starts to bubble, turn to lowest setting. Cover and cook (simmer) for about 20 minutes.
3. Sprinkle cheese on top and eat right out of the pan. Or you can be a little classier and pour beans into a bowl and serve with chips.

*Tip: For an easy way to "mince" fresh garlic, see illustrations on page 123.

Bean Dip

Serves 2 to 4
45 minutes

Saucepan with Lid
Stovetop

Bell Pepper Strips

Serves 12
5 minutes

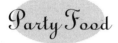

Broiler Pan
(lined with aluminum foil)

Oven Set at Broil

INGREDIENTS:
- 1 GREEN BELL PEPPER, seeded and cut into 6 strips*
- 1 RED BELL PEPPER, seeded and cut into 6 strips*
- 1 YELLOW BELL PEPPER, seeded and cut into 6 strips*
- 1 ½ cups shredded MONTEREY JACK CHEESE
- 1 4-oz. can CHOPPED RIPE OLIVES
- sprinkling CRUSHED RED PEPPER

DIRECTIONS:
1. Cut bell pepper strips crosswise in half.
2. In broiler pan, lay pepper strips close together and cover with cheese, olives, and red pepper.
3. Set oven control to Broil. Broil peppers within 3 to 4 inches from heat for about 3 minutes, or until cheese is melted. *Watch carefully.* Cheese can burn quickly under broiler heat.

*Tip: See illustrations for cutting bell peppers on page 122.

INGREDIENTS:

- MAYONNAISE (use according to number of bread slices)
- PUMPERNICKEL BREAD slices (as many as you want)
- 1 CUCUMBER, very thinly sliced
- dash LEMON PEPPER or "Lawry's" SEASONED SALT
- FRESH PARSLEY, finely chopped

DIRECTIONS:

1. Spread mayonnaise over each slice of pumpernickel bread.
2. Cut bread slices small enough to fit the sliced cucumber (or use cookie cutter for various bread shapes).
3. Add one slice of cucumber to every piece of bread.
4. Add a dash lemon pepper on cucumber.
5. Sprinkle with chopped parsley.

Display on tiered tray for an impressive table at social events.

Serves 12
10 minutes

Serving Tray

"Instant Party" Cheese Dip

Serves 6 to 8
3 minutes

Party Food

INGREDIENTS:
- 1 round 12-oz. container SOFT CREAM CHEESE
- ½ cup SALSA (hot or mild, your choice)
- couple shakes of "Tabasco Green" JALAPEÑO SAUCE
- bag TORTILLA CHIPS

DIRECTIONS:
1. Place container of cream cheese upside down on serving plate. Tap until cheese slides out of container onto plate.
2. Pour salsa over cheese.
3. Shake jalapeño sauce over top. Use liberally if you like it spicy.
4. Serve with flavored tortilla chips. Colorful and delicious.

Serving Plate

INGREDIENTS:

- 1 RUSSET POTATO, scrubbed to remove all dirt, unpeeled
- 1 tablespoon "Miracle Whip" SALAD DRESSING
- sprinkle ONION SALT
- dash BLACK PEPPER

DIRECTIONS:

Preheat oven to 375°.

1. Cut potatoes lengthwise into thick strips.
2. Brush the strips with salad dressing.
3. Place on aluminum foil. Sprinkle with seasonings.
4. Bake for 50 minutes, or until tender and golden brown.

Potato Sticks

Serves 1
50 minutes

Heavy Aluminum Foil
(rubbed with vegetable oil to
prevent sticking)
375° Oven

Wine Cheese

Makes 1 cup
5 minutes

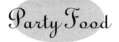

INGREDIENTS:
- 1 8-oz. package CREAM CHEESE
- 1 teaspoon MINCED ONION FLAKES
- 2 tablespoons HORSERADISH SAUCE
- 1 teaspoon WORCESTERSHIRE SAUCE
- ¼ cup WHITE WINE
- PARTY CRACKERS (your choice)

DIRECTIONS:
1. Dump all ingredients except crackers into a small mixing bowl and stir well with a spoon until smooth.
2. Shape into a ball and place on center of a large plate.
3. Surround with party crackers.

Small Mixing Bowl

Large Plate

Delicious Drinks

INGREDIENTS:
- ½ cup APPLE JUICE
- 3 scoops VANILLA ICE CREAM or FROZEN YOGURT
- ½ teaspoon GROUND CINNAMON

DIRECTIONS:
In blender, add apple juice and ice cream. Blend on high until well mixed. Stir in cinnamon.

Simple, easy, and delicious!

Serves 1
5 minutes

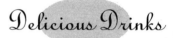

Blender

Chocolate Milk Shake à la Tofu

Serves 1
5 minutes

Delicious Drinks

Blender

INGREDIENTS:
- 4 oz. FIRM TOFU
- ½ 8-oz. container VANILLA YOGURT
- 1 BANANA
- 7 ICE CUBES
- 2 tablespoons HOT COCOA MIX
- ½ cup MILK
- ½ cup WATER

DIRECTIONS:
1. Dump all ingredients into blender.
2. Blend on high speed until smooth and creamy.

INGREDIENTS:
- 1 BANANA
- handful FROZEN STRAWBERRIES
- 1 cup ORANGE JUICE
- 4 oz. FIRM TOFU
- spoonful HONEY

DIRECTIONS:
Dump all ingredients into blender and blend until smooth.

Try a variety of fruit, but use some form of frozen fruit to give a thickness to this smoothie.

Fruit Tofu Smoothie

Serves 1 to 2
3 minutes

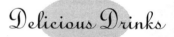

Blender

Old-Fashioned Lemonade

Serves 1
5 minutes

Delicious Drinks

Blender
Tall Drink Container with
Tight-fitting Lid

INGREDIENTS:
- CRUSHED ICE (*Fill blender jar with ice cubes. Turn on high speed and crush. Drain off excess water and use.*)
- 1 cup cold WATER
- 1 large LEMON, cut in half
- 1 tablespoon SUGAR or 1 packet LOW-CALORIE SWEETENER

DIRECTIONS:
1. Dump crushed ice into tall container.
2. Fill to top of container with cold water.
3. Squeeze juice from lemon over ice and sprinkle with sugar.
4. Place lid on jar tightly and shake vigorously for a *full minute*.

Lemon Aids:

How to get more juice from a lemon: Roll lemons until slightly soft before squeezing and you'll get a lot more juice out of them.

How to keep fruit from discoloring: Squirting a little lemon juice on cut-up fruit, like apples, pears, bananas, etc., will help keep them from discoloring.

INGREDIENTS:
- 1 cup cut-up MELON*
- 1 8-oz. can CRUSHED PINEAPPLE
- 10 FROZEN STRAWBERRIES
- 1 cup ORANGE JUICE
- 7 ICE CUBES

DIRECTIONS:
1. In blender jar, dump all ingredients in the order given.
2. Cover jar and blend on high speed until smooth and icy.

Melon Freeze

Makes 2 cups
8 minutes

Delicious Drinks

Blender

*Tip: This is a good recipe to use up any leftover pieces of melon.

Mocha Cappuccino Freeze

Serves 1
3 minutes

Delicious Drinks

Blender

INGREDIENTS:
- 1 cup MILK
- 2 teaspoons INSTANT COFFEE
- 1 cup CHOCOLATE ICE CREAM (or your favorite)
- sprinkle CINNAMON SUGAR (See page 3.)

DIRECTIONS:
In blender, mix together milk and instant coffee. Add ice cream and blend until smooth. Sprinkle cinnamon sugar over top and enjoy!

INGREDIENTS:
- 4 oz. FIRM TOFU
- ½ 8-oz. container PEACH YOGURT
- 1 BANANA, cut up
- 1 PEACH, cut up
- ⅓ cup FRUIT JUICE (pineapple, apple, etc.)
- ⅔ cup WATER
- 7 ICE CUBES

DIRECTIONS:
1. Dump all ingredients into blender.
2. Blend on high speed until smooth.

Tofu Peach Smoothie

Serves 1 to 2
3 minutes

Delicious Drinks

Blender

Index

ALSO AVAILABLE FROM WARNER BOOKS

THE STARVING STUDENTS' COOKBOOK
by Dede Hall

Anyone can learn to cook simple, filling, nutritious, and tasty meals—all on a student's budget and schedule. *The Starving Students' Cookbook,* the classic bestselling guide for the clueless gourmet, will show you how. Featuring 150 delicious, foolproof recipes, cooking tips, and easy-to-follow directions for healthy meals that can be made on the quick and cheap, this book is required reading for every semester—whether you're in school or out of it!

THE OCCASIONAL VEGETARIAN
by Karen Lee with Diane Porter

Renowned cooking teacher and author Karen Lee gives you this sumptuous cornucopia of over 200 meatless recipes. Whether you're a strict vegetarian or someone who still enjoys a steak now and then, you'll be truly satisfied by these robust, healthy alternatives to the old meat-and-potatoes style of eating. More than just a cookbook, *The Occasional Vegetarian* shows you how to organize meals and "build" feasts that are sure to please both full- and part-time vegetarians.

30 LOW-FAT VEGETARIAN MEALS IN 30 MINUTES
by Faye Levy

You can cook it tasty . . . cook it fast . . . and cook it *100 percent vegetarian.* It's easy with Faye Levy's 100 low-fat, low-cost, fast-fixing, and boldly seasoned vegetarian dishes. Here are recipes that focus on pasta, beans, rice and other grains, one-pot menus, soups, salads, and fruit desserts—all bursting with flavor. Faye will guide you step by quick step through irresistibly delicious and healthy menus that will save you time and money!